Thinking Medieval

Also by Marcus Bull:

FRANCE IN THE CENTRAL MIDDLE AGES 900–1200 (*editor*)

KNIGHTLY PIETY AND THE LAY RESPONSE TO THE FIRST CRUSADE

THE MIRACLES OF OUR LADY OF ROCAMADOUR

Thinking Medieval

An Introduction to the Study of the Middle Ages

Marcus Bull

First published 2005 by
PALGRAVE MACMILLAN
Houndmills, Basingstoke, Hampshire RG21 6XS and
175 Fifth Avenue, New York, N. Y. 10010
Companies and representatives throughout the world

PALGRAVE MACMILLAN is the global academic imprint of the Palgrave
Macmillan division of St. Martin's Press, LLC and of Palgrave Macmillan Ltd.
Macmillan® is a registered trademark in the United States, United Kingdom
and other countries. Palgrave is a registered trademark in the European
Union and other countries.

ISBN-13: 978-1-4039-1294-7   hardback
ISBN-10: 1-4039-1294-7   hardback
ISBN-13: 978-1-4039-1295-4   paperback
ISBN-10: 1-4039-1295-5   paperback

This book is printed on paper suitable for recycling and made from fully
managed and sustained forest sources.

A catalogue record for this book is available from the British Library.

Library of Congress.Cataloging-in-Publication Data
Bull, Marcus Graham.
    Thinking medieval : an introduction to the study of the Middle Ages /
    Marcus Bull.
        p. cm.
    Includes bibliographical references and index.
    ISBN 1-4039-1294-7 (cloth) — ISBN 1-4039-1295-5 (paper)
        1. Middle Ages—Study and teaching. 2. Civilization, Medieval—Study
    and teaching. 3. Middle Ages—Historiography. 4. Medievalism. I. Title.

D116.B95 2005
909.07—dc22

                                                        2005051167

10   9   8   7   6   5   4   3   2   1
14   13   12   11   10   09   08   07   06   05

Printed and bound in Great Britain by
Antony Rowe Ltd, Chippenham and Eastbourne

For Sasha

CITY AND COUNTY OF SWANSEA LIBRARIES	
Bertrams	18.11.07
940.1	£14.99

Contents

Acknowledgements

I would like to thank the following for their help, advice and suggestions, some going back several years and others very recent: Tom Asbridge, Malcolm Barber, Brenda Bolton, Fergus Cannan, James Clark, Jean Dunbabin, Penny Galloway, Ben Herman, Norman Housley, David Jones, Richard Lambert, Catherine Léglu, Christoph Maier, Jonathan Phillips, Catherine Pitt, Philip Richardson, Jonathan Riley-Smith, Brendan Smith, Felicia Smith, Ian Wei, and Beth Williamson. To my wife Tania and my daughter Sasha I owe everything for their love and support.

Introduction: What is 'Thinking Medieval'?

This book is aimed at students and general readers coming to the study of medieval history for the first time, as well as at those with a background in other branches of medieval studies who are interested in finding out a little about historians' aims and perspectives. This is not a brief history of what happened in the Middle Ages or of the development of the medieval historical profession. Nor is the book intended to be a contribution to the currently fashionable debates about the nature of history and history-writing (although the present author's own position on some of these debates will be implicit in parts of the discussion). Rather, the book aims to set the scene for the study of medieval history by placing it in a wider context as a cultural phenomenon, a collection of inherited labels, a scholarly methodology, and, like all academic subjects, something that needs to justify itself in what we are increasingly encouraged to regard as the educational 'market place'.

The four chapters that follow are designed to anticipate a sequence of questions that someone might ask as she or he begins and then gets deeper into the study of the Middle Ages for the first time. To start with, even before the first class is attended and the first textbook opened, it is useful to ask 'What do I already know about the Middle Ages?' To this end, Chapter 1 looks at some of the images and preconceptions about medieval civilization that have become part of modern popular culture. To 'think medieval', in other words, is to ponder what the words 'Middle Ages' and 'medieval' have come to mean beyond the academic context. What associations do these terms trigger, and why? The aim of the chapter is not to trivialize academic study by claiming that it and popular culture stand in some sort of equal relationship. Far from it. But it is important to be aware of the ways in which the two things overlap and interact, especially because this helps us to avoid many of the pitfalls that await someone thinking about a distant and alien historical subject such as medieval Europe. Chapter 1 therefore explores some of the ideas about medieval life, many but not all of them negative, that have become part of the Western world's cultural baggage. In particular, it focuses on the period between the later eighteenth century and the beginning of the twentieth when many of our current ideas about the Middle Ages either first appeared or, if older, entered the cultural mainstream. Although some consideration will be given to much more recent manifestations of the pop-cultural take on the Middle Ages, such as the movie *Pulp Fiction*, which came out in 1994, there would be little point in devoting the whole discussion to the very latest films, television shows, electronic games, toys, advertising and all the other media in which references to the medieval period can be found. The result would be a list of up-to-the-minute cultural referentia which would date very quickly. In fact, what one finds is that the latest pop-cultural appropriations of things medieval are almost always variations on well-worn themes, even when the specific medium, such as a computer game, is a recent phenomenon. To understand something of the roots of these familiar themes, then, is to equip oneself to contextualize whatever bits of the Middle Ages that pop culture is seizing on at any given moment.

'Thinking medieval' can also be about reflecting on the origins and usefulness of the categories that underpin historical debates about the Middle Ages. The next stage, then, is to ask how the terms 'Middle Ages' and 'medieval' came into being. Chapter 2 explores the ways in which the 'middleness' of the Middle Ages was created between the fourteenth and nineteenth centuries, while also offering some thoughts on the pros and cons of historical periodization more generally. People in the Middle Ages did not think of themselves as 'medieval', of course: the word could only be coined later, by people looking back in time and using the past to reinforce value judgements about their own culture and civilization. The chapter argues that in an ideal world we should jettison the labels 'Middle Ages' and 'medieval' altogether: not only do they come burdened by five centuries or more of judgementalism, they block off a chunk of historical time which is too unwieldy and too internally diverse to be a useful unit of analysis. For now, however, we are stuck with the terms, which means that we should always be aware of the many problems that they create. In fact we can turn this around to our advantage because being alive to the pitfalls of periodization can help us to frame new and more searching questions about the parts of the past that interest us.

To 'think medieval' is also to ask how, in a very basic sense, we are in a position to know anything about the Middle Ages in the first place. Chapter 3 therefore asks what sort of evidence survives from medieval Europe, and how it influences what historians can or cannot say. This chapter is not a comprehensive survey of all the various types of sources. In fact, one of the points to stress is that the variety and volume of evidence surviving from the Middle Ages, especially after about 1200, are such that it is reductive and misleading to talk about 'medieval sources' as a single overarching category. If we do, this becomes another way of falling into the trap of supposing that the 'Middle Ages' denotes a real and distinct historical entity, as discussed in Chapter 2. Some medieval source types are carry-overs from the ancient world, others continue past 1500; even source types that are entirely medieval, in the sense that they are only found somewhere within the 500–1500 period, are very unlikely to fill the whole of that span. So, rather than run through lists of the main types of primary evidence, the discussion focuses on some of the reasons why written sources, which are most medieval historians' staple resource, have survived; and, equally, why we have lost a great deal of material. Primary sources are not simply the means to the ends of historical analysis; they are a fundamental part of the story itself. Nowhere is this more true than with medieval history, so even at an early stage in one's exploration of the subject, it is important to be alive to some of the possibilities that sources open up and the constraints that they impose. To 'think medieval' without 'thinking sources' is impossible.

Finally, to 'think medieval' is to reflect on the value of studying the history of the Middle Ages. Once one has got some way into the nitty-gritty of the subject, some of the key terms, events and processes, it is reasonable to ask what it all amounts to. What is it for? What looks like a fairly straightforward, if large, question actually subsumes a very wide range of problems. On one level, thinking about the value of studying medieval history is one small part of a much broader debate about the role of education and learning in our modern culture, our whole civilization no less. Clearly, this is a topic beyond the scope of a book of this sort. On a more manageable level, the importance of medieval history resides in its being one element – still small, but now proportionately more noticeable – within the full range of arts and humanities subjects that are taught and researched in educational institutions. Chapter 4 begins by offering some thoughts on this level of debate, particularly in relation to the charge of uselessness (whatever that in fact means) sometimes brought by outsiders pursuing a variety of agendas, be they politicians playing to public prejudices, or scientists and other specialists in purportedly 'useful' subjects. More specifically, however, the most helpful way to think about the importance of medieval history is in relation to the criticisms sometimes voiced by insiders: that is to say, other scholars such as historians of more recent parts of the past who are implicitly persuaded of the value of studying the arts and humanities in general terms but who like to choose the relative merit of different slices of history by appeal to the criterion of 'relevance'. Most of Chapter 4, therefore, takes up this particular issue, on the assumption that if one can make a good case for medieval history's relevance (again, whatever that means) in relation to other branches of academic history, then satisfactory answers to the bigger issues about humanities subjects in general, and academic endeavour across the board, can be constructed by mobilizing the example of medieval history as part of the wider argument.

'Relevance' is a slippery concept meaning different things to different people, which is precisely why accusations of irrelevance can be so hard to defeat to the complete satisfaction of the accuser. Rather than talk about relevance in abstract terms, therefore, Chapter 4 offers some thoughts on this debate by focusing on two case studies. The first, the history of the English language, has been chosen because it is something which clearly relates to how many millions of people today go about their lives. As we shall see, the period between the end of Roman rule in Britain (one workable if old-fashioned way of marking the end of ancient civilization and the emergence of the medieval in that part of the world) and the end of the fifteenth century was of formative significance in the creation of what we would nowadays recognize as English. In the year 500 'English' as such did not exist; the best we can say is that there was a cluster of related West Germanic dialects which would utterly baffle us if we heard them spoken. By 1500, we are only two or three generations shy of Shakespeare, and the English of the period, if not always very easy, is recognizably the same sort of thing that we use today. To this extent, then, English was 'made in the Middle Ages' – more so, in fact, than other European languages whose different chronologies of development have a less obviously medieval fit. The Middle Ages are thus demonstrably relevant if one wishes to understand something as fundamental to our current experience as the language we speak. On the other hand, the chapter goes on to argue that we can easily overplay the relevance card: various arguments counsel caution, and these apply not just to the English language, probably the most pervasive and omnipresent legacy of the Middle Ages to be found in modern anglophone societies, but also to any aspect of medieval life which finds some echo or continuity in our contemporary experience.

The second case study is the crusades, the holy wars that have acquired a particular resonance as a result of current political and religious tensions, especially since 9/11. Chapter 4 argues that attempts to mobilize the crusades in modern-day rhetoric, both Western and Muslim, are at best misconceived and at worst specious. The crusades are, in fact, an excellent demonstration of the distortions and illogicalities that always flow from trying to squeeze relevance out of the Middle Ages contrary to what is historically accurate or intellectually valid. They are an object lesson in the limitations of the concept of relevance when it comes to justifying the study of the Middle Ages. The mindsets of the people who conceived, planned and went on crusades were fundamentally different from our own assumptions and values. They were not 'like us' only more thuggish and intolerant. What this exposes is that the issue of relevance is often based on a profound misconception: that there are powerful continuities between how people in the distant past and people now think and behave, with the necessary implication that the ways in which people thought and behaved then have a direct, linear bearing on what we are and do today.

In fact, as Chapter 4 goes on to argue, the relevance of medieval people is precisely the fact they were not like us at all, however many superficial similarities might emerge in some of the evidence. In other words, the value of studying medieval history, its relevance if you like, is not about making facile causal connections over long reaches of time, but about getting to grips with the fact of difference, or 'alterity' to give it a technical quality. The Middle Ages are relevant because they present fascinating and, yes, difficult challenges. It really comes down to plain intellectual excitement, and to respect for the extraordinary diversity of human experience. That is about as good a definition of historical relevance as any, and it neatly brings us back full-circle to the issues raised in Chapter 1. A major flaw in pop-cultural images of the Middle Ages is that, while they naturally allow for the existence of external trappings different from our own, often in order to convey messages about the exotic or grubby quality of medieval life, they tend to underestimate the internal, mental differences between medieval people and ourselves. At best medieval people become caricatures of the qualities that we welcome or shun when we encounter them in the modern world. But it is always wise to assume difference unless and until there is some evidence for similarity, not the reverse. This is essentially what makes medieval history so interesting – and so relevant to any historical education.

For the purposes of the discussion, the terms 'medieval' and 'Middle Ages' largely refer to the civilization and culture of western Europe between about 500 and 1500. This is not meant to downplay the importance of eastern European history in this period, nor of contemporary non-Christian cultures, in particular medieval Judaism and Islam. These are among the growth areas of medieval studies in recent years, to the immense benefit of the whole discipline. In practical terms, however, an emphasis upon western Europe makes sense because it remains the core element of most introductory courses and textbooks. The medieval West is also, as we shall see, the screen onto which nearly all our pop-cultural images of medieval civilization are projected, just as it supplied the main yardstick against which Renaissance thinkers and later writers came to measure the 'middleness' of medieval life.

Notes and suggested reading

Notes are confined to supplying the references for direct quotations. For bibliographical guidance, readers are directed to the Suggested Reading section, which is arranged by chapter, with subdivisions that follow the thematic sequence in the text.

1
Popular Images of the Middle Ages

No one can come to the formal study of history with a mind like a blank sheet of paper. We are already conditioned to engage with the past by the culture that surrounds us. The past – or, to be more accurate, a selection of highlights from the past – is embedded in Western popular culture in a host of ways. This has implications for our understanding of history even as we aim for the levels of sophistication and complexity that academic study demands. Academic history sometimes tries to project an image of detachment, situating itself above the busy swirl of popular culture. It is often said, with some justice, that one of the benefits of studying history to an advanced level is that it equips people to see through all the misconceptions and half-truths about the past that exist in the public domain. On the other hand, the idea of scholarly detachment can also be taken too far. When this happens, it can quickly descend into pious posturing which severely underestimates the significance of popular culture in all our lives. Exposure to popular culture is not 'wrong' or detrimental to your scholarly health. It is not something to be sheepish about as one enters the hallowed portals of academe. Popular culture accounts for some of the instinctive curiosity that makes us interested in history. And it is one of the ways in which we practise thinking about the past and how we stand in relation to it.

Nor is popular culture detached from academic history in a more formal sense. Some historians would argue that there is a trickle-down effect which enables scholarly ideas to seep into the popular consciousness, although this will usually have a built-in time lag, with the result that popular understandings often end up as approximations of once-fashionable but now rather outdated academic interpretations of the past. Other historians are less convinced that this sort of connection routinely exists. They prefer to argue that popular ideas about the past are mostly generated from within the cultures that accommodate them, like modern-day versions of ancient folklore. In fact both arguments have merit. Ask people where they think they have got their ideas about the past from, and the response is likely to be a combination of many sources, some of them more obviously academic in origin, others broadly popular. Possibilities include family traditions, memories of children's stories, pictures in the schoolroom, the remarks of a history teacher, school textbooks, exposure to elite culture in the form of outings to museums and galleries, tourism, toys and games, novels, television and film, advertising and many other influences. It will usually be impossible for someone to trace a particular notion about some aspect of the past back to a specific source: instead, it will just feel like an obvious part of the cultural scheme of reference, part of the mental furniture.

What this means is that the academic study of history does not exist in isolation from other ways of thinking about the past, although the connections are complex and variable. Although a phrase such as 'popular culture' is very useful, it should always be remembered that it is really a huge oversimplification. The term is shorthand for an enormous variety of perspectives and degrees of complexity, some nudging towards what we associate with academic discourse, others operating on a much more simplified and populist level. No two people assemble identical mental scrapbooks of the bits of the past that have meaning for them, even when they come from similar social, educational and cultural backgrounds. For these reasons, when embarking on the formal study of a historical period such as the Middle Ages, it is very important to keep at least half an eye on the popular cultural dimension. This can enhance our historical understanding, and it reminds us that, just as we each have our own individual take on the mix-and-match past on offer in popular culture, so we also have something to contribute individually to the academic study of history, by thinking for ourselves, weighing up different ideas and posing challenging questions. Popular culture, in other words, equips us to be more thoughtful and informed about the past.

The fact is we are surrounded by the past. We are bombarded with it in numerous ways. History, for example, is a fertile terrain for advertisers and designers. Architects can quote from the past in their plans for buildings. In the world of journalism, the ability to see the long view, that is to contextualize current affairs by looking back into the past, is regarded as a mark of judgement and depth. Museums and sites of historical interest solemnize the past but also make it part of the world of leisure and entertainment. The heritage industry employs many thousands of people. A notable feature of how modern Western culture packages the past is its taste for an eclectic mix of different periods, places and civilizations. Numerous electronic games, for example, create worlds in which the key visual markers such as costume and armour, technology and architecture, are a hotch-potch taken from multiple sources. Sword-and-sorcery fantasy favours the same sort of mix, as does science fiction, which, though set in the future, regularly plunders the past for its images and ideas. This eclecticism is not just a feature of lower-brow culture. Visitors to a historic country house, for example, are seldom presented with the remains of just one tightly-framed place and period. Their normal experience is to encounter a variety of images and artefacts from different times and locations; these cumulatively create the sense of the 'pastness' communicated by the place, something that cannot be pinned down to a particular year, decade or sometimes even century.

Our love for the mix-and-match past is seen by some cultural commentators as a symptom of our supposed postmodern condition. That is to say, we have abandoned our faith in history as progress, as a sort of straight line stretching from then to now, so instead we now play with the past, treating it like a giant shopping mall full of images, motifs and ideas which we can consume in whatever combinations we choose. There may be some truth in this view, but it is important to remember that running different parts of the past together and getting things mixed up are not recent inventions: one comes across something similar, for example, in a twelfth-century epic loosely based on events in the eighth century, or in a thirteenth-century Arthurian romance set in a distant past that we would nowadays locate sometime around the sixth century. The only difference is that in our contemporary society our cultural repertoire of bits and pieces from the past is much larger and more diverse than ever before.

Popular perceptions of the past may be a jumble, but that is not the same as saying that they are in complete chaos. A great deal of selection and ordering is always going on, even though we are seldom aware of it. There are many historical periods and places that register very little, if at all, as cultural reference points. And not all the pieces of the past that make it into the popular consciousness do so on equal terms. Some bits of the past are quite precisely drawn and very specific in their cultural significance. Others are much broader and more open-ended; they are like mood-music playing in the background, as opposed to a single memorable tune. The Middle Ages fall into this second category. In part this is because people will often be dimly aware, even if they think they know nothing else about the medieval period, that it lasted a long time. But sheer duration cannot be the whole story. The civilization of ancient Egypt lasted many centuries and was rich and diverse, but its place within popular culture nowadays is as a very compacted range of images and associations. One thinks, for example, of pyramids, temples, pharaohs, Tutankhamun's gold mask, mummies, mummies' curses, hieroglyphic writing, and Cleopatra. The repertoire of associations is small but potent, and very importantly each element seems to reinforce the validity of all the others, or at least not to undermine it. In this way, what we think we are getting from the interlocking elements is an internally consistent vision of what ancient Egypt was 'like'. To some extent the same applies to popular images of classical Greece and Rome.

In stark contrast, the Middle Ages are altogether harder to pin down. They feel much looser around the edges. Although there are powerful associations tied up with medieval Europe, as we shall see, no one set of associations is so dominant that it lends the time and place the clarity with which we think we can picture ancient Egypt. There are no iconic moments of discovery for the Middle Ages on a par with the finding of the Rosetta Stone, which unlocked the mystery of the hieroglyphs, or the opening of Tutankhamun's tomb by Howard Carter. There is no medieval Pompeii frozen in time under volcanic ash. The Middle Ages feel closer to us in some ways, but that only makes it more difficult to see them in the round. To explore the place of the medieval period in modern popular culture, therefore, involves locating several different strands of ideas and images, not all of which fit neatly together.

An excellent, if at first sight unlikely, place to start our investigation is a movie with a most unmedieval setting, the drug- and violence-fuelled underworld of 1990s Los Angeles. Any list of cult classics in modern cinema would have to include Quentin Tarantino's *Pulp Fiction* (1994). All the writer-director's signature techniques are on display in this controversial and powerful movie. There is the elaborate interweaving of separate plot lines, and the playful breaking up of chronological sequence. There is plenty of Tarantino's trademark violence, which always hovers somewhere been the artfully stylized and the disturbingly realistic. And of course the film positively fizzes with modern cultural references, the disposable 'pulp' of film, television, music and all the bits and pieces of modern consumerist living. The references are often very allusive – a throwaway remark, a film showing on the television in the background of a scene, the music soundtrack. At one point in the film one of the main characters, played by Samuel L. Jackson, declares that he has had a religious conversion. He will walk the earth like Caine, he says, a reference that only takes on meaning if one can recall the basic plot device of the early 1970s television series *Kung Fu*. The barrage of cultural references, most of them deliberately very fleeting, amounts to a knowing invitation to the audience to feel included, to get the point. Popular culture, in its very nature, has a short and insecure chronological reach, a theme that Tarantino explores by setting a key scene in Jack Rabbit Slim's, a Fifties-themed diner where the staff are dressed up to look like cultural icons such as James Dean and Buddy Holly. The character played by Uma Thurman mistakes the waitress impersonating the minor starlet Mamie Van Doren for the much more famous Marilyn Monroe. When she is corrected by her companion, played by John Travolta, we feel that here is someone (like Tarantino himself, in fact) with an unusually good grasp of material on the outer fringes of popular cultural reference. This is as far back as I can take you, Tarantino is saying; this is where the sort of past we truly need has its origins.

In the light of the built-in obsolescence of the sorts of trivia that Tarantino simultaneously celebrates and junks, it is striking to note that, right in the middle of the riot of references to the very recent and the evanescent, the film includes one mention of a much more distant time, the Middle Ages. A complex series of plot twists conspires to place two of the main characters, the boxer Butch Coolidge (played by Bruce Willis) and the gangster Marsellus Wallace (Ving Rhames), in the clutches of three murderous sadomasochists. Butch kills one member of the gang and makes his escape, but, in a fit of conscience, he goes back to help Marsellus even though Marsellus wants him dead for failing to throw a fight as they had arranged. Once the second sadomasochist has been violently dealt with, leaving the third alone and mortally wounded, Marsellus agrees to let Butch off the hook provided he gets out of town fast. For his part, Marsellus says he will stay behind in the basement torture chamber to which they had been taken, promising to get help from certain associates who will bring 'a pair of pliers and a blowtorch'. Turning to his victim, Zed, Marsellus declares, 'Hear me talkin', hillbilly boy? I ain't through with you by a damn sight. I'm gonna git medieval on your ass!' Beyond the assurance that this will involve 'agonizing pain', Marsellus does not care to elaborate. The expression registered on Butch's face shows that he understands perfectly well what

Marsellus is getting at, and by extension the audience too is invited to use its imagination to fill in the gaps. Tarantino has slipped in another brief but resonant cultural reference. The action cuts to Butch leaving the building, and we leave Zed to his unseen but no doubt utterly appalling fate. As Butch later tells his girlfriend, 'Zed's dead, baby, Zed's dead'.

In truth, this description sanitizes what is in fact a breathtakingly violent passage in the film, complete with murderous weapons, brutal assault, sexual torture, male rape, and psychological abuse. So the brief and apparently casual mention of 'medieval' towards the end of such a sequence is all the more remarkable. It becomes code for the unseen, even more awful climax to follow. Tarantino has spotted something very deep-rooted and visceral in the associations that a word such as 'medieval' is able to trigger in people's minds. Bloody, bleak, unrestrained, barbaric, physical, unthinking, brutal, dark, ominous: these sorts of adjectives get us close to the associations that are compressed within Marsellus's brief utterance.

Moving from blood to froth, one finds a similar range of associations at work in Michael Crichton's book *Timeline* (1999), an attempt to do for the Middle Ages what the same author did for dinosaurs in *Jurassic Park*. (In fact, the movie version, which came out in 2003, was terrible and duly bombed.) In the book, a brilliant but malevolent scientist-cum-entrepreneur has invented a machine that can transport people back in time, and the book relates the adventures of a group of young academics and students as they try to rescue their Yale history professor, who has gone missing in fourteenth-century France. Authorially, Crichton affects the posture of someone who knows what he is talking about. He claims to have done a lot of solid research; the book in fact includes a very respectable bibliography of scholarly work on the Hundred Years War. Some of the period detail is decently if superficially handled. The book is all good, lightweight stuff, true airport reading, but that is what makes it interesting. One of the reasons why Crichton's books and films have usually been commercially successful is because they tap into some of modern society's vulnerabilities and fears: resurrected dinosaurs, rogue technologies, unfamiliar cultures, and deadly diseases all challenge our cosy assumptions about our ability to dominate our world. With this in mind, it is significant that in *Timeline* Crichton drops his time-travelling heroes into a world that is particularly nasty and brutish. And short. Pretty much the first thing that happens to the rescuers when they arrive in 1357 is that one of them is beheaded by a mounted assailant for no apparently obvious reason, and another is riddled with arrows. 'The suddenness of it,' one of the heroes thinks to himself, 'the casual violence.'[1] More of the same crops up again and again later; we get blood-soaked fights to the death as well as revealing little vignettes of the ugliness of medieval life, such as when a knight petulantly amuses himself by stabbing a dog with his knife (which he then uses to eat his meal).

Thus far we have encountered 'medieval' essentially as a synonym for 'brutal', but, as the example of *Timeline* helps to show, the word resonates because it encapsulates something more than just a disapproving response to a physical act of violence. The word is also saying something about a whole range of values and ways of behaving which, rightly or wrongly, are projected onto the Middle Ages. That is why Marsellus's use of 'medieval' works so well as code: it creates meaning in the audience's mind by triggering a chain reaction of associations, evoking not just the fact of extreme violence, but also the sort of people who were (supposedly) capable of that violence, and by extension the sort of society that could have produced those people in the first place. It amounts, then, to a form of social comment in which a caricature of the past is held up to the present in order to form a contrast or to make a point about some underlying similarity.

The point to stress here is that there is nothing intrinsically odd about using something like the Middle Ages as a way of talking about aspects of our modern experience. We do this sort of thing all the time; the language we speak and write is littered with metaphors, similes and analogies, and we are constantly describing one thing with reference to something else quite different. Sometimes the comparisons we make work because although on a literal level they appear inappropriate, they get around the problem by wearing their inappropriateness very openly. This creates something akin to an in-joke to be shared by speaker and listener. But there is nothing joking or ironic about the uses of 'medieval' that we have identified. There is no playful twisting around of natural meaning such as we find in the slang use of 'bad' to mean 'good'. For Tarantino, Crichton and their audiences, the connection only works if, yes, the Middle Ages really were that bad!

It is for this reason that one finds the word 'medieval' cropping up in contexts that are far more real and serious than pop-culture books and movies. An excellent example is the trial in the international court in The Hague of the former Yugoslav president Slobodan Milosevic. Milosevic was accused of crimes against humanity that had been committed as his regime struggled throughout the 1990s to resist separatist forces in Croatia, Bosnia and Kosovo. The grim term 'ethnic cleansing' entered the language to euphemize the regime's atrocities, including the murder of thousands of Bosnian Muslims at Srebrenica in 1995. When the trial began, in February 2002, the chief United Nations prosecuting attorney, Carla Del Ponte, used her opening address to describe the actions of Milosevic's troops as instances of 'almost medieval savagery and a calculated cruelty that went far beyond the bounds of legitimate warfare'.[2] The 'almost' is a chilling touch and speaks volumes. Del Ponte's choice of language was in fact consistent with what had already become a stock way of thinking about the situation in the former Yugoslavia as some sort of reversion to a more primitive age. The Swedish politician and diplomat Carl Bildt, who as a peace envoy tried, largely unsuccessfully, to end the bloody warfare in Bosnia, has regularly registered his exasperation with people he describes as inhabiting a narrow, medieval world of injustices, revenge and continual struggles.

It is striking how embedded the word 'medieval' and its associated images have become in informed, educated discourse. A serious newspaper such as *The [London] Times* regularly returns to the theme. Take, for example, the newspaper's coverage in the first few weeks of 2003: this is a useful sample period precisely because it was unexceptional, there being no big story that raised public awareness of the Middle Ages unusually high or made 'medieval' a particularly fashionable buzzword. We find that the Middle Ages crop up in variety of contexts. For example, a commentator reflecting on the assassination by an animal rights activist of Pim Fortuyn, a right-wing Dutch politician, argues that, by whipping up public feeling against Fortuyn, the liberal Dutch press had been virtually complicit in his murder. 'But why,' the commentator wonders, 'did they [Dutch journalists] feel such a powerful need to act like medieval villagers screaming for heretics to be burnt at the stake?'[3] Another think-piece ponders the treatment meted out to Michael Jackson in an infamously unsympathetic television documentary, one that Jackson claimed had been shot under false pretences by a film crew feigning friendship and support. 'There was something almost [that qualifier again!] medieval about the ritual by which he was cut down. First came the worship, then the unmasking, and finally the casting into outer darkness.'[4] Medieval associations seem such a good way to set a tone, to turn on the mood-music in the reader's mind, that they get wheeled out in contexts where the risk of anachronism should properly counsel extreme caution. For instance, another piece in *The Times* reports how a group of Orthodox monks on Mount Athos in Greece was protesting against their patriarch's friendly dealings with members of other Christian denominations. The journalist clearly wants to register that there is something very deep-rooted and primitive about the monks' fanaticism. 'In what could have been a scene from the Middle Ages, Father Methodios [the rebels' leader] brandished what he said were photographs of Patriarch Bartholomew giving communion to Catholics and Protestants.'[5] Two anachronisms, then, for the price of one.

Awareness in academic terms of what the Middle Ages were like is clearly not a big issue in these examples. A picture of villagers screaming for heretics to die is overdrawn to the point of cartoon caricature, and it scarcely amounts to a representative image of medieval civilization. The scene itself is just about conceivable, although it runs counter to our knowledge of how heretics were usually dealt with by the authorities. Heretics in fact evoked a wide range of responses from the people they encountered; many people were in fact supportive. Quite what, if anything, lies behind the imagery summoned up in the other two pieces in *The Times* is still more baffling. But what is clear is that the sorts of associations that we have identified in the context of violence are in fact only part of a more complicated and nuanced picture. To summon up the ghost of the Middle Ages works for the writers of these pieces, and for their readers, because 'medieval' triggers a range of negative associations: primitiveness, superstition, small-worldism, bigotry, fearfulness, irrationality, superficiality, inflexibility and intolerance. And not a redeeming quality in sight.

Denigration of the Middle Ages does not always have to take the form of crash-bang condemnation in order to be effective. Sometimes more subtle and layered treatments can stick the knife in every bit as well. Take, for example, Mark Twain's book *A Connecticut Yankee at King Arthur's Court* (1889), which recounts the adventures of a New England factory superintendent who is knocked unconscious and transported back to Britain in the year 513, the time of King Arthur. The precision in the date, it should be noted, is potentially misleading: the story is not set in the sixth century as modern scholarship would understand that period. On the contrary, the reader is taken back to an imprecise, all-purpose medieval era which, to judge from Twain's evocations of it and from the numerous engaging illustrations by Dan Beard that accompanied the first edition, is a combination of pure fantasy and realistic detail applicable to different phases of the Middle Ages. The centre of gravity is towards the later end of the period, especially the fifteenth century, but no clear sense of chronological consistency emerges. The probable historical basis for the mythical figure of King

Arthur was a Romano-British warlord operating in the sixth century, so to this extent Twain was on the right lines. But the setting of *A Connecticut Yankee* places it in a tradition of indifference to problems of anachronism that goes back to the founding father of Arthurian literature, Chrétien de Troyes. Chrétien's romances were set in the physical and mental spaces of his own world, northern France in the later twelfth century. Thanks to the popularity of later medieval reworkings of the Arthurian legends such as Thomas Malory's English version *Le Morte d'Arthur* (c.1470), the dress, armour and architecture of the fourteenth and more especially the fifteenth century have become canonical as suitable Arthurian trappings. Any later, of course, and it would stop looking medieval! Alfred, Lord Tennyson's popular blank-verse adaptation of Malory, *Idylls of the King* (published in sections between 1859 and 1885), as well as the numerous Victorian paintings inspired by the interest in things Arthurian that Tennyson helped to stimulate, draw on this late medieval setting. More recently, the same has been true of cinematic treatments such as the film version of the Lerner and Loewe musical *Camelot* (1967), John Boorman's superior, Malory-inspired *Excalibur* (1981), and the dull *First Knight* (1995). Even movies which try to make something of being set in a late Roman twilight, such as the very poor *King Arthur* (2004), actually end up mimicking the style and substance of late medieval Arthuriana. Firmly within this venerable tradition of chronological blurring, Twain's treatment of Arthur's Britain is not specifically directed at the 'darkness' of the early medieval Dark Ages. A much broader, all-inclusive vision of the Middle Ages is at stake.

The book's central character, Hank Morgan, is a technocrat brimming with belief in the importance of science and the superiority of modernity. Exploiting his late nineteenth-century know-how, such as when he uses dynamite to outdo the 'magic' trickery of the king's advisor Merlin, Morgan works his way into a position of political mastery. At the same time he attempts to drag society into the modern world, introducing, amongst other trappings of 1880s modernity, newspapers, the telegraph and bicycles. On a superficial level Morgan's collision with medieval culture comes across as a celebration of all the advances that mankind has made since the Middle Ages. Most modern critics would argue, however, that there is more to the book than this. If Twain's purpose had been simply to celebrate the marvellous accomplishments of his own age compared to those of earlier periods, then the sort of Middle Ages that he constructs would have been much too soft a target – a non-target, if anything, scarcely worth making the basis of a book. In fact, Twain would seem to be offering a critique of the destructive power of modern technological progress as well as of the backwardness of medieval society. Significantly, the book ends indecisively, not with the triumph of the new over the old, but in an unnecessary and bloody battle which destroys both Morgan's vision and the forces of reaction that range against him.

Arthurian Britain, it should be noted, is not presented as an entirely alien culture. Morgan is able to relate to people and to distinguish different traits and qualities in them. He is able to recruit a team of sympathizers to support him in his modernization drive. And he even gets married. On the other hand, this does not mean that the book pulls its punches when it comes to criticism of the Middle Ages. Apart from Morgan's enlightened accomplices, people are locked into their ignorance. They unquestioningly accept social inequality and the imposition of hierarchy. They lack the mental equipment to make change happen; in one important chapter Morgan is utterly frustrated in his attempts to explain some very basic economics about the relationship between earnings and spending power. What Twain anachronistically calls the 'established' church keeps everyone in thrall to superstition and fear. People are like children in their simplicity. Worse still, they are 'modified savages', a particularly revealing term when one recalls that White American attitudes towards Native Americans were a live issue when Twain was writing. So, for all the shadings and nuances in Twain's vision, the basic qualities of the Middle Ages are its backwardness and the fact that it is static. (This of course begs the question what could have happened between then and 1889 to break the mould and bring Morgan's modern world into being, but this is not a problem that Twain's stark contrast between past and present has to address.)

The sorts of ideas that we have been encountering, not least Mark Twain's bitter hostility towards religious superstition, show how much attitudes since the nineteenth century have owed to eighteenth-century Enlightenment thinkers such as Voltaire (1694–1778) and Edward Gibbon (1737–94). The Enlightenment worshipped reason and the idea of human progress, and this relegated the Middle Ages to an inferior position in its historical vision. The Middle Ages were seen as a period in which mankind was prevented by barbarism and superstition from realizing its full potential. Religion had been the tool of an overmighty Church that protected its power by keeping people in ignorance. The poverty of the many had put a brake on change. Violence had been rife, a symptom of a flawed civilization that was unable to keep itself under proper control. Of course, Western thought and culture have moved on in many different directions since the Enlightenment (which was not in fact the homogenous movement that the term implies). But it still exerts a strong influence on modern-day sensibilities. Consider, for example, the frequently made, if not particularly helpful, observation that Islamic fundamentalism exists because the Muslim world has not been through its own version of the Enlightenment, which, the argument goes, would have created the sort of separation between religion and secular affairs that Western societies take for granted. Despite coming under attack in recent decades, belief in the value of reason and hope in the possibility of progress remain important parts of many people's view of the world. The catch is that respect for the values of the Enlightenment tends to mean buying into its vision of an earlier, darker age, a time when our primitive side was to the fore. This then becomes the benchmark against which we measure how much we have improved our lot in recent centuries.

This helps to explain why it is negative ideas about the Middle Ages that predominate in popular culture. Things are not quite so simple, however. We are also the heirs of more positive interpretations which likewise date back to the eighteenth and nineteenth centuries and have also filtered through into popular perceptions. The result is that we are presented with competing, and sometimes irreconcilable, visions. A good illustration of this point is the varied career and interests of William Morris (1834–96). Morris, who came from a privileged if not aristocratic background, grew up absorbing the Romantic medievalism offered by the novels of Walter Scott (which we will discuss in detail later) and stories of King Arthur. At Oxford, he and his close friend Edward Burne-Jones toyed with the idea of founding a monastic community. Soon afterwards he entered the circle of Dante Gabriel Rossetti and the Pre-Raphaelite Brotherhood of artists, who were strongly influenced by medieval civilization. In the 1860s he helped to found a company dedicated to the making of medieval-style furnishings and fittings using medieval craft techniques. He also campaigned against the destruction and unsympathetic restoration of medieval buildings. In all these things Morris might simply appear to have been a representative of mainstream nineteenth-century medievalism, which was generally reactionary in tone. But one of the most interesting aspects of Morris's life is that his politics moved to the left in the later part of his career without his jettisoning his love for the Middle Ages. On the contrary, his understanding of what medieval life had been like became central to his wider political vision.

This is demonstrated above all in his *A Dream of John Ball* (1888), like the closely contemporary *A Connecticut Yankee* a dream-and-time-travel encounter between the medieval and modern worlds, but very unlike Twain's book in its positive appraisal of medieval (specifically fourteenth-century) conditions. For Morris, the late Middle Ages had been a golden, if sadly brief, period in which the peasants in the countryside had been prosperous, and in the towns the guilds, or self-regulating craft associations, had protected workers from exploitation, thereby releasing them to find satisfaction in the creative possibilities of their work rather than having to churn out inferior products for someone else's profit. Modern opinions about Morris tend to be mixed: he was either a hero of the early labour movement, or the inventor of champagne socialism, according to taste. He was also fairly unusual in his left-leaning medievalism. But he is important because he helps to show how the nineteenth century's interest in the Middle Ages was not hitched to a single vision of the world. This meant that when the political and social debates that fuelled medievalism at that time gradually lost their currency, enthusiasm for the Middle Ages did not just dissipate with them. The residue for us nowadays is a raft of images and associations largely freed from their earlier polemical charge, and now available to us in different combinations according to our desires and needs.

One way in which the Middle Ages can be appropriated to satisfy modern concerns, and something which is likely to become even more evident in the future, is the fashioning of an image of medieval civilization as a pre-industrial idyll, a time when people supposedly lived in harmony with their environment. This view has a long pedigree. Perhaps its earliest and most influential exponent was William Cobbett (1763–1835), whose many writings, especially his *A History of the Protestant Reformation in England and Ireland* (1824–6) and *Rural Rides* (1830–2), evoked a charmed rural England that was being destroyed by the forces of industrialization and agrarian change. For Cobbett this lost idyll was not specifically medieval; it was as recent, and as tantalizingly just out of reach, as his grandparents' generation and his own apple-pie memories of childhood. But the Middle Ages supplied the ballast, the centre of gravity, of his thinking because they represented the quintessential pre-industrial era. It is easy to see how the same sorts of ideas might be attractive today, as we fret about global warming and pollution. Weren't the Middle Ages a simpler, more harmonious time, when people respected nature? In fact, this notion is one of the easiest medieval stereotypes to debunk. Over the course of the medieval period enormous changes were made to the environment: vast swathes of forest were felled, marshlands drained, coastlines altered. It was simply the technology available, not some mushy sense of being in touch with nature, that limited the rate of change.

In contrast to the image of rural calm beloved of Cobbett and others, there has also been a long tradition of talking up the supposed grimness and unpleasantness of medieval culture. The aim is not to be turned off by the Middle Ages but to find in them something compelling and attractive. This can be linked back to the work of the 'Graveyard Poets' around the middle of the eighteenth century, followed towards the end of the century by the emergence of the Gothic novel. Much of the bric-a-brac of modern bats-in-the-belfry horror can be traced back to these genres – foggy graveyards, ruined and mysterious castles, the ghostly clanking of chains, dark omens and portents, superstitious peasants, moaning monks, torture chambers, and sinister underground passages. What is sometimes called the first Gothic novel, Horace Walpole's *The Castle of Otranto* (1764), is set in twelfth- or thirteenth-century Italy (not that there is any concern for accurate period detail as we would now understand it). Later Gothic writers took up Walpole's interest in southern Europe, in part because its Catholicism and its half-familiar, half-exotic feel created a compelling mix of attraction and distaste in northern Protestant readers.

In terms of the choice of chronological settings, however, the debt to Walpole was less marked. The stock repertoire of Gothic motifs was not uniquely or indeed necessarily medieval in its associations; the action in many of the most popular and influential Gothic novels, such as Ann Radcliffe's *The Mysteries of Udolpho* (1794) and *The Italian* (1797) and Matthew Lewis's *The Monk* (1796), takes place in what we would now call the early modern period, between the sixteenth and eighteenth centuries. On the other hand, the general tone and evocation of period feel – castles, aristocratic power, superstition, pronounced social distance between the powerful and the servile, the institutions of monasticism, a sinister and malevolent Catholic church – could easily be projected further back in time to the Middle Ages proper. This was reinforced by the popularity of contemporary German terror-writing, which tended to be set more squarely in what we would understand as the medieval period. The Middle Ages, capable of being broadened out by a couple of centuries because southern Europe was imagined as backward and so still in a way medieval, seemed the right sort of setting for stories taking place in an age of, in Walpole's words, 'miracles, visions, necromancies, dreams, and other preternatural events'.[6] Thanks to Walpole's influence on the Gothic novel and then to the Gothic novel's influence on wider visions of the medieval, it is the sort of setting that still proves compelling to numerous writers, game designers and movie makers.

Viewed in isolation, the taste for the supernatural and the macabre to be found in Gothic novels looks like the standard hostility towards the Middle Ages, its supposed superstition and disorder, only dressed up as melodrama. But the popularity of works such as *The Castle of Otranto* was not solely down to a taste among the reading public for having all its worst prejudices about the Middle Ages confirmed. On the contrary, their appeal was one aspect of a growing interest in medieval civilization which sought to redress the starkly negative view of the Middle Ages favoured by many influential Enlightenment writers. This quickening of interest and positive reappraisal can be detected in the final third of the eighteenth century. It became progressively more pronounced in the first half of the nineteenth century, peaking around 1850 but remaining a significant cultural trend for several decades thereafter, perhaps until as late as the First World War.

The revival of interest was evident in many media, including poetry, prose literature, painting, and the theatre. One of the most important was architecture. Architectural history nowadays tends to be fenced off as a specialist discipline, with the result that it seldom features as prominently as it should in 'mainstream' history. It is easy to underestimate the cultural significance that has been attached to architecture in the past. In the eighteenth and even more in the nineteenth century, an appreciation of architecture was seen as central to an understanding of an entire civilization. The idea was that buildings contained more than the obvious clues about the manner of their construction – the structural principles informing the design, the raw materials used, the location relative to other structures, and so on. A building was also able to communicate the broader values of the society that created it: most obviously ideas about aesthetics because some buildings at least were meant to be beautiful, but also more general social and cultural values, prevailing notions of spirituality, and even trends in political thought. Research into the past often seeks out key 'diagnostics', that is to say particular characteristics and processes that are believed to throw light on the bigger picture, just as when medical symptoms visible in one part of someone's body can tell a doctor about the patient's overall condition. Architecture enjoyed this sort of diagnostic status in the medieval revival from the later part of the eighteenth century (as indeed, as we shall see in Chapter 2, it had provided one of the ways in which Renaissance thinkers defined their 'modernity' in relation to the medieval past).

An excellent illustration of architecture's importance in the medieval revival is Victor Hugo's novel *Notre-Dame de Paris*, published in 1831.

(Since the time of the first translations of the book in the mid-1830s, the standard English version of the title has been *The Hunchback of Notre Dame*, which is inaccurate but is at least luridly memorable.) In this novel the cathedral of Notre-Dame in Paris is more than an impressive backdrop for much of the action. It is almost like a living character. It expresses the values and habits of mind of a whole civilization, a civilization that at the time in which the novel is set, 1482, is succumbing to a new and modernizing order represented by the figure of King Louis XI. Hugo served on committees dedicated to the preservation of France's old buildings, and he wrote articles fulminating against the architectural 'vandals' who were tearing down medieval structures in towns across France in the name of progress and profit. Because old buildings were the most visible and public vestiges of the medieval past in many parts of nineteenth-century Europe, but were also under particular threat from urban and rural redevelopment as populations increased and shifted, it is easy to see why architecture was an obvious battleground for advocates of all things medieval.

Some of the most impressive medievalist polemics have architecture as their theme. In *Contrasts* (1836), for example, Augustus Welby Pugin, most famous today as one of the architects of the British Houses of Parliament, presented pairs of facing illustrations depicting comparable scenes, one from the fourteenth and fifteenth centuries, and the other, starkly contrasting, image from the nineteenth. The best known pairing juxtaposes a late medieval monastery tending to the needs of the poor, who are well looked-after and dignified, even in death, with the hunger, rags and degradations of the victims of a modern workhouse, who end up as corpses being carted away for dissection. The use of medieval/modern architectural contrasts as the leitmotif for contemporary social criticism was taken further by John Ruskin in his *Stones of Venice* (1851–3). Medieval buildings, he argued, had been made by men who had a stake in their work and took pride in it, something which made them truly free and close to nature and God. On the other hand, modern workers had been turned into alienated, dehumanized robots.

As these examples show, medieval architecture was of interest to sophisticated thinkers because it reinforced their use of the Middle Ages as a metaphor for the social and cultural changes that they wanted to see in their own day. But architecture could also satisfy the tastes of those whose enthusiasm for the Middle Ages needed more literal and tangible forms of expression. From around the middle of the eighteenth century there developed what is now termed the 'Gothic Revival', a movement which spawned countless buildings that were inspired by medieval prototypes, in particular by churches and castles. Big buildings of this sort survived from the Middle Ages much more than modest domestic structures, which tended not to have been built to last centuries or, if they did survive, were usually submerged under hundreds of years of rebuilding work. So it was high-cost, high-prestige 'public' buildings like cathedrals and fortresses that impressed themselves most forcefully on people's imaginations. An interest in medieval buildings had a long history; in England, for example, almost as soon as Henry VIII sold off the dissolved monasteries' estates and the purchasers began to tear down monastic buildings for raw materials or to convert them to secular uses, there were people who found the 'bare ruined choirs' an evocative reminder of a lost age. But it was not until the eighteenth century that sensitivity towards medieval architecture turned into a desire to mimic it.

As with the Gothic novel, a key early figure was Horace Walpole. In the 1750s and 60s he had Strawberry Hill, a house that he had recently bought in Twickenham south-west of London, 'gothicized' inside and out, complete with battlements and turrets, stained glass and cloistered passages. (The building substantially survives, and is now part of a university.) By around 1800 many people with, like Walpole, the money to pursue their medievalist dreams were converting their houses in the same ways or having new medieval-style homes built from scratch. This vogue was to last a century or more. It is easy to scoff at some of the more ludicrous expressions of the Gothic craze, especially in its early decades when, as was the case at Strawberry Hill, a lot of the work was more about show than substance, with the result that papier mâché crenellations rotted away, canvas towers blew away in storms, and designer ruins simply fell down. Perhaps the most revealing example is a vast Gothic pile, Fonthill Abbey, built in Wiltshire by William Beckford, a rich libertine and, interestingly, another Gothic novelist. The centre-piece of Fonthill was an extraordinary tower nearly 300 feet in height, but the materials used were so poor and the foundations so shallow that it came crashing down – twice! Beckford was not alone, however. A lot of people put a lot of money into medievalist architecture, which is significant in itself, and the results became both better built and more authentic. It is also noteworthy how often representatives of 'new money', people with no aristocratic pedigree who had made their fortunes from industry or commerce, bought into the medievalist dream by building Gothic mansions for themselves.

More significantly still, the craze for Gothic architecture was not limited to the private dwellings of the privileged. From the early part of the nineteenth century it developed a more public and communal face. Most of the churches built in British towns, and significant numbers in North America and on the Continent, especially Germany, were medieval in inspiration. For the most part, architects and their clients looked back to the Gothic style of architecture which emerged in northern France around the middle of the twelfth century and came to dominate ecclesiastical architecture in Europe north of the Alps up to the fifteenth century (and in some places later still). What most people know about Gothic is that its signature motif is the pointed arch, in contrast to the typical rounded arch of the 'Romanesque' period that preceded it. More broadly Gothic represented the achievement of light and height as opposed to the squat solidity of Romanesque structures. It is important to note, however, that the 'Gothic' revival was more elastic and variegated than the name might seem to suggest, and this was an important reason for its success. Different architects favoured different phases within the Gothic period as the ideal to which to aspire: the decades leading up to 1300 were often held up as the time when Gothic architecture had reach the peak of perfection, but there were champions of earlier and later manifestations of it. In addition, Romanesque was a significant additional source of inspiration, favoured in Germany, for example, as a model for new Protestant churches in order to distinguish them from Catholic designs. Crucially, then, the Gothic Revival avoided the sort of monotony which would have made its impact much shorter and more superficial. Many churches are very good copies of medieval prototypes, so much so that one sometimes hears people expressing surprise to learn that a familiar landmark church which they had always imagined dated from the Middle Ages, because it 'looked right', is in fact a Victorian creation.

To transpose medieval forms into modern ecclesiastical architecture made perfect sense, of course, because the survival of so many original medieval churches created a feeling of continuity and parallelism. The taste for very slavish adherence to medieval models peaked around the middle of the nineteenth century. But, very importantly, Gothic proved a very flexible and adaptable style, with the result that buildings could easily incorporate many features associated with the medieval without having to be stone-by-stone copies. Gothic likewise adapted to unmedieval building materials such as iron and concrete. This enormously broadened people's exposure to medievalist architecture, and enabled medieval motifs to be transplanted comfortably into settings where there was little or no continuity with actual medieval life. The result is that in many places today we come across medieval-style town halls, school buildings, law courts, prisons, factories, libraries, cemeteries, war memorials, railway stations and post offices. On a day-to-day basis, these sorts of structures probably account for most people's routine exposure to anything even remotely connected to the Middle Ages, so their effect on our impressions about what medieval life must have been like should not be underestimated.

The taste for creating mock-medieval buildings ran alongside a growth in interest in the lifestyles and values of the people who had lived in the medieval originals. It was taken for granted that men were more important than women, and there was also a leaning towards the history of people from the higher social levels, so it is not surprising that particular attention was paid to the ideas and values of medieval aristocratic males. That meant, of course, the code of chivalry. Early and influential treatments include Jean-Baptiste de la Curne de Sainte-Pelaye's *Mémoires sur l'ancienne chevalerie* (1750–2) and Richard Hurd's *Letters on Chivalry and Romance* (1762). These helped to redress the hostile Enlightenment caricature of chivalry as hollow folly. They spread the image of the medieval knight as physically brave, noble, steadfast, generous, loyal to his superiors, responsible towards his subordinates, and considerate towards women. Chivalry as seen in these more positive terms had a twofold effect: by appearing to be anchored historically in the medieval past, chivalry felt real rather than a set of values that was impossibly ideal; and this made it seem particularly attractive and relevant to latter-day aristocrats and their admirers. If the eighteenth-century renewal of interest in chivalry began as a way for *ancien régime* patricians to celebrate their class identity, the French Revolution raised the stakes. Chivalry became a leitmotif of the sort of social and political order that opponents of the Revolution wanted to restore, or a lament for a lost world beyond recovery. In the famous words of the conservative thinker Edmund Burke in his *Reflections on the Revolution in France* (1790), 'But the age of chivalry is gone. That of sophisters, oeconomists, and calculators, has succeeded; and the glory of Europe is extinguished for ever.'[7] It is significant that one of the most influential discussions of medieval chivalry in the post-revolutionary years was in the writings of François-René de Chateaubriand (1768–1848), especially his *Génie du christian-isme* which appeared in 1802. Chateaubriand came from an aristocrat-ic Breton family which fared very badly in the Revolution: his father's remains were dug up by revolutionary zealots, and his mother and sister were thrown into prison, where the poor conditions wrecked their health. Chateaubriand himself spent several years in exile in the

United States and England. Little wonder, then, that 'the time of chivalry', as he called the Middle Ages, became for him a symbol of the good old days when energetic and responsible, that is, chivalric, aristocrats had ruled over a well-ordered and harmonious society.

The man who did more than anyone else to popularize the image of the chivalrous knight was Sir Walter Scott (1771–1832), whose 'Waverley Novels' (so called after the first in the sequence, published in 1814) created an enormous appetite for historical fiction in Britain and abroad. Scott and his works scarcely register in modern-day surveys of people's favourite authors or best-loved books, but during his lifetime and for many decades afterwards he was without doubt a literary superstar. He had the knack of being able to fill his narratives with lots of interesting and evocative detail. Not all of this detail stands up to historical scrutiny today, of course, but in its day it was a real eye-opener when compared, say, to the sort of hazy inattention to historical specificity that people were getting in many Gothic novels. Although only about a quarter of Scott's novels have medieval settings (he was particularly drawn to the history of Scotland around the time of the Jacobite uprisings), it was with the Middle Ages that he became particularly associated, mainly thanks to his most popular novel, *Ivanhoe*, which was published in 1819.

Scott had great timing. After the final defeat of Napoleon in 1815 and the end of two decades of European war, the old certainties seemed to have gone. The adventures of Scott's chivalrous heroes and the triumphs of the chivalric values that they espoused helped people to adjust to an unsettling peace, in much the same way that American, Japanese and British culture explored its reactions to the end of the Second World War through the movies. Scott's stories can seem very corny today. In particular, modern readers are often struck by how one-dimensional and wooden the central knightly characters appear. Wilfred of Ivanhoe in *Ivanhoe*, the eponymous hero in *Quentin Durward* (1823) and Sir Kenneth the Leopard Knight in *The Talisman* (1825) seem much less engaging than the other character types, especially the women, outsiders such as Jews and Muslims, people of low status and, of course, the villains. But this is largely the result of changes in literary taste and sensibility, and we should not underestimate the appeal and influence of Scott's knightly characters in his own time. It has been calculated, for example, that no fewer than 74 paintings inspired by *Ivanhoe* and 25 inspired by *The Talisman* were exhibited between the mid-1820s and the mid-1840s at the Royal Academy, the main showcase for established and aspiring British artists. Scott's novels were adapted for the stage. They were translated into other languages: one of the reasons why Victor Hugo was moved to write *Notre-Dame de Paris* was his experience of reading *Quentin Durward*, likewise set in the France of Louis XI. In Gustave Flaubert's *Madame Bovary* (1856–7), we are told that the heroine Emma had read Scott as an impressionable fifteen-year-old in smalltown Normandy:

> From Walter Scott, subsequently, she conceived a passion for things historical, dreamed about coffers, guard-rooms and minstrels. She would have liked to live in some old manor-house, like those chatelaines in their long corsages, under their trefoiled Gothic arches, spending their days, elbow on the parapet and chin in hand, looking out far across the fields for the white-plumed rider galloping towards her on his black horse.[8]

Scott spawned numerous imitations that further fixed the image of the chivalric hero in people's minds. Nor is it fanciful to suggest that later cultural incarnations of the values of the medieval knight in cowboy and action movies owe a great deal to Scott's vision.

One of the most revealing indications of Scott's hold on people's imaginations was the Eglinton Tournament. This was an odd case of life imitating art, for one of the big set-piece scenes in *Ivanhoe* is a tournament at Ashby-de-la-Zouche. In June 1838 the coronation of Queen Victoria was a low-key, cost-cutting affair light on pageantry and pomp, a fact which grated with many members of the aristocracy. By way of compensating for what they felt was their marginalization, a group of aristocrats and fellow travellers, led by Archibald Montgomerie, Earl of Eglinton, started to plan some form of medieval costume pageant. In due course this expanded into a Scott-esque tournament involving mounted knights charging at one another in the lists. Samuel Pratt, a London businessman who made his money feeding the demand for the mock-medieval, supplied the armour, which to judge from contemporary illustrations was based on fifteenth- and early sixteenth-century designs. After much more planning and organization than had been originally anticipated, the tournament took place in the grounds of Eglinton Castle in August 1839. More than a hundred people had showed some initial interest in being knights, but in the event only fourteen took part, adopting grandiose titles such as the 'Black Knight', the 'Knight of the Golden Lion' and the 'Knight of the Burning Tower'. The supporting cast was much larger, however, including ladies led by the 'Queen of Beauty', servants and retainers in costume, actors and entertainers.

The thing that everyone came to remember about the Eglinton Tournament was that it was a complete disaster. Heavy rain drenched everyone, the tournament arena turned into a mudbath, and the whole affair descended into chaos. Although the organizers managed to salvage something from the wreckage by staging a replay two days later, the abiding image of the fiasco that became lodged in people's minds was of men grandly dressed up as medieval knights but cowering under their very modern umbrellas. For many the incongruity of this image summed up the silliness and pomposity of the whole idea. Critics of the craze for things medieval were delighted to be gifted such a target. To some extent, of course, the Eglinton Tournament was about a few privileged people with the money and time to indulge their historical fantasies. But for the purposes of our discussion, a much more significant point is that the event generated an enormous amount of interest among members of the general public. It was estimated that the tournament attracted one hundred thousand spectators, including significant numbers from abroad. These sorts of numbers would only be found at the biggest sporting events even today; in the first half of the nineteenth century they were truly remarkable. Many people joined in the spirit of the occasion by wearing medieval costume, much of it making up in enthusiasm what it lacked in historical accuracy. Eglinton was off the beaten track, about twenty miles from Glasgow in a quite remote part of south-western Scotland. To get there most people relied on travelling by train and steamboat. These were both very new transport technologies which would not have been available even a few years earlier. An act of homage to the distant past, the Eglinton Tournament was, paradoxically, one of the first demonstrations of the new world of mobility that the industrial age was opening up. The fact that the tournament generated so much enthusiasm is ultimately more important than the fact that this enthusiasm was largely frustrated. It shows that popularizers such as Sir Walter Scott had made an enormous impact in raising the profile of the Middle Ages.

Those who had written to the organizers of the Eglinton Tournament to ask for tickets included a Lieutenant Gore of the United States Navy and a Mr B. F. Babcock from New York, who although 'being...somewhat a stranger' was 'anxious with a few lady friends from the United States to witness the sports'.[9] Clearly enthusiasm was not confined to the Old World. Yet this raises larger questions about how the Gothic Revival and the increased interest in the Middle Ages played in America. How did Americans respond to medievalist ideas given that they were so bound up with the European experience? A lot more was at stake than the simple fact that the United States felt itself to be a very new nation, whereas the Middle Ages all seemed so very long ago. Political ideology and an emerging sense of national identity inevitably sharpened attitudes. After all, the United States as a political experiment was grounded in Enlightenment ideas about progress. The Constitution was construed as a rejection of the monarchical tyranny that was seen as the norm in European states; and the Declaration of Independence and the Bill of Rights offered people precisely the sorts of freedoms and opportunities that were supposedly denied those trapped in backward-looking and hierarchical social systems.

This could cut both ways. The British arch-champion of medieval chivalry Kenelm Digby, whose *The Broadstone of Honour* (first published in 1822 and reissued in various expanded versions over the next fifty or so years) was an enormously influential handbook of gentlemanly behaviour based on medieval examples, hated Americans simply for being democratic! It is significant that post-revolutionary America favoured neoclassical buildings that expressed the values of the ancient Greek city-state and Republican Rome; the idea of a 'Capitol', after all, comes from the prototype building on the Capitoline hill in ancient Rome. Gothic buildings would have sent out quite the wrong messages: castles evoked aristocratic privilege, medieval-style churches the idea of an official state religion, both anathema to the Founding Fathers. The expansion of American society and its absorption of new waves of immigrants in the nineteenth and early twentieth centuries, though it profoundly changed America in many ways, actually helped to re-inforce post-revolutionary attitudes towards the Middle Ages. Many of the new migrants were people escaping religious and ethnic persecutions in various parts of Europe. Their negative memories of the Old World, coupled with their gratitude for having a new life, helped to create the (still widely held) American image of Europe as a place riven by implacable and ancient hatreds. Because the Middle Ages seemed to supply many of the historical myths that fuelled these hatreds and injustices, they were necessarily implicated as part of the negative and divisive 'Other', in contradistinction to which a positive and inclusive American self-image could be fashioned.

More than this, there was a serious problem of chronological symbolism. The story of America was generally believed to begin with part of the transition – if not, indeed, *the* moment of transition – between the medieval and modern worlds, that is to say Columbus's first voyage of discovery to the New World in 1492. This was seen as much more than a coincidence. On the contrary, if it could be claimed that it was precisely the discovery of America that had brought the curtain down on the Middle Ages, then American history could be seen to acquire extra meaning as a distinctively 'post-medieval' tale, with all that this implied for rejecting the baggage of the feudal past. The vision of American origins enshrined in influential books such as Washington Irving's *Life and Voyages of Christopher Columbus* (1828) played on the notion of a virginal land that had lain untouched and, crucially, unnamed during the medieval centuries. (This, of course, blithely disregarded thousands of years of Native American history!) So powerful was this vision that it downplayed the one bit of European medieval history in which America could claim some direct involvement: the adventures of early eleventh-century Vikings from Greenland who explored parts of what are now the Canadian and New England coasts and went ashore in several places, encountering some Native Americans and attempting to establish permanent settlements, though without success. There were staunch supporters of the Norse claim to have discovered America, but the prevailing mood was to stick with the Columbus story, so much so that a group of Norse enthusiasts were moved to gatecrash the 1893 Chicago Exposition, which was themed around the celebration of the four-hundredth anniversary of Columbus's discovery, by building a replica Viking ship and launching it on a lake within sight of the exhibition stands!

Yet, in spite of all these factors working against enthusiasm for the Middle Ages, it is striking how much interest in things medieval still managed to spread in North America. In part this was because the political elites in the United States saw aspects of medieval European history, in particular the development of representative institutions and common law in medieval England, as their own prehistory. Famously, an early design for the Great Seal of the United States, which was not in the end adopted, featured Hengist and Horsa, the two mythical leaders of the Anglo-Saxon invasion of Britain in the fifth century. As American society diversified in the nineteenth century, and the political dominance of patrician Protestants of northern European descent came under pressure, this attachment to the supposed Anglo-Saxon connection was fortified as a way of dealing with unwelcome change. The interest in the Viking past owed something to the same impulse.

There was much more to the American enthusiasm for the Middle Ages, however, than the easing of the anxieties of worried WASPs. Interest in the Middle Ages developed in many of the same ways and fastened on the same sorts of medieval motifs as in contemporary Europe. Chivalry would always be a big attraction, of course. It used to be generally supposed, for example, that the white gentry of the antebellum South was particularly susceptible to Walter Scott's romanticized vision of medieval chivalry because it found within it many reflections of its own code of values. An extreme piece of evidence to support this connection appears in Mark Twain's *Life on the Mississippi* (1883), in which he describes his experiences during a visit to the South in the mid-1870s. Twain thought he saw the baleful influence of Scott everywhere. In language anticipating the theme of his *Connecticut Yankee* a few years later, he wrote:

> The South has not yet recovered from the debilitating influences of his [Scott's] books. Admiration of his fantastic heroes and their grotesque 'chivalry' doings and romantic juvenilities still survives here, in an atmosphere in which is already perceptible the wholesome and practical nineteenth-century smell of cotton-factories and locomotives; and traces of its inflated language and other windy humbuggeries survive along with it.[10]

Later on he becomes even harsher when reflecting on the stunted growth of 'practical, common-sense, progressive ideas' in the South:

> Then comes Sir Walter Scott and his enchantments, and by his single might checks this wave of progress and even turns it back; sets the world in love with dreams and phantoms; with decayed and swinish forms of religion and degraded systems of government; with the sillinesses and emptinesses, sham grandeurs, sham gauds, and sham chivalries of a brainless and worthless long-vanished society. He did measureless harm; more real and lasting harm, perhaps, than any other individual who ever wrote...But for the Sir Walter disease, the character of the Southerner...would be wholly modern, in place of modern and mediaeval mixed, and the South would be fully a generation further advanced than it is...Sir Walter had so large a hand in making Southern character, as it existed before the [American Civil] war, that he is in great measure responsible for the war.[11]

No historian today would go along with Twain's rhetorical flourish about the causes of the Civil War, and modern analysis of antebellum Southern society tends to be guarded in the significance it attaches to medievalism, pointing out that White Southern values were much less uniform and straightforward than the idea of a medieval inspiration implies. Nonetheless, it is clear that many Southerners did find within

the Middle Ages (or rather the bits they chose to see) congenial parallels with their own experience, and this helped to reinforce their self-
image. 'Cotton snobs' appealed to chivalric ideals of honour, gentlemanly decorum, social leadership, hospitality, military prowess, horse-
manship, and respect for women. Some 'ring tournaments' (shows of
equestrian skill so called because one of the exercises involved getting
the point of a lance through a suspended rope ring) were dressed up in
medieval trappings; an event staged at the Virginian spa resort of
Fauquier Springs in 1845, for example, included trumpeters, heralds,
and armour-clad knights with names taken from *Ivanhoe*. The chivalric
theme also extended into political discourse. As tensions built up
between the North and the South in the years before the Civil War, it
became common for Southerners to think of themselves as the descendants of the aristocratic, refined, chivalrous 'Normans', whereas the
hated Yankees were descended from lower-status Puritans whose ances-
try went back to churlish, money-grubbing, anti-chivalric 'Saxons'.

If the American interest in things medieval had been confined to
the old South, we might now look on all this very much in the past
tense and as a case of one faded civilization clinging to the memory of
another. But in fact medievalism's impact was much more widespread. Even supposedly 'Saxon' New Englanders could be drawn to
the chivalric myth: one of the forerunners of the Boy Scout movement,
for example, was an organization founded in Vermont in 1893, the
'Knights of King Arthur', whose members met around a Round Table
and imagined themselves part of a world of knightly honour. Arthurian
stories became popular in the nineteenth century across America, and
the appetite for them in books, games and films remains very strong.
It is significant that when people wanted to find a word to capture
the new mood of optimism that they associated with the presidency of
John F. Kennedy (1961–3), 'Camelot' seemed the perfect name for the
glamorous White House 'court'.

Medievalism extended into other media. From around the middle
third of the nineteenth century, Gothic architecture became more
popular, sometimes going off in new and eclectic directions because it
was freed from the constraints imposed on architects in Britain, where
people could always make comparisons with medieval originals just
down the road. For example, Eastern State Penitentiary in Pennsylvania,
begun in the 1820s, was modelled on Downton Castle, an eighteenth-
century building in Ludlow, but it was also a state-of-the-art prison
design accommodating the latest thinking about how to deal with criminals. In a more frivolous vein, the same spirit of copying-but-adapting

links the designs of the iconic castles in the Disney theme parks to the mock-medieval castles commissioned by nineteenth-century German princes, most famously Neuschwanstein built for Ludwig II of Bavaria (1845–86). One of the things that got Mark Twain so worked up was coming across the Louisiana state capitol in Baton Rouge, which bucked the trend of neoclassical governmental buildings by being designed on Gothic lines. Many American students today are familiar with Gothic buildings: Harvard's Memorial Hall and Princeton's University Chapel are early examples of a style that has been copied on many campuses. The Washington National Cathedral (begun in 1907, and not finished until 1990) is another impressive witness to the attraction of Gothic, all the more significant for becoming a landmark in a city which was originally designed as a neoclassical statement in stone. The cathedrals of Notre-Dame and Christ Church in Montreal and the Houses of Parliament in Ottawa are imposing examples of the importance of Gothic across the border in Canada.

The fact that nineteenth-century medievalist enthusiasms were able to take root in North America, in spite of the contrary forces that we have identified, has significantly affected how we think about the Middle Ages today. If the New World had turned its back on the Middle Ages entirely, it is possible to imagine a situation in which medieval history would have become an even more recherché subject than it actually is. It would probably be of parochial interest to a few people in those countries with the obvious medieval connections, but its narrow geographical range would no doubt have had the effect of reinforcing the sense of its chronological remoteness. The main reason why this has not happened is that American enthusiasm for the medieval has helped to 'universalize' the Middle Ages, turning them into part of our global historical narrative and giving them a significance which transcends the story of what happened in one fairly small extremity of the Eurasian landmass a long time ago, before the world turned modern. Pioneers of academic medieval history like Henry Adams (1838–1918), the first medieval history professor at Harvard, were able to get the Middle Ages onto the university curriculum by exploiting the tension between familiarity and detachment that characterized American attitudes towards the medieval. We shall see in Chapter 4 that the old confidence in medieval European history as a proper part of the history taught in schools and universities is now under severe strain as the venerable 'grand narratives' of history are questioned and unpicked. But in the context of popular culture that is our present concern, we find that precisely this same sort of tension – between something that

feels wild and unsettling while at the same time familiar and domesti-
cated – still runs through North American attitudes towards the
medieval. This is in turn reflected in the enormous influence that
America has on popular culture elsewhere in the world, including of
course those parts of the Old World where medieval history 'came
from' in the first place.

A good case study which draws together many of the themes that we
have been considering is the story of the image and reputation of the
Vikings. The Vikings are worth looking at in some detail because they
occupy a prominent place in popular perceptions of the earlier part of
the Middle Ages, that is to say, what people imagine was the rough,
tough, barbarian Dark Age phase. Their image, moreover, spills over
into contexts which are far from limited to what the Vikings actually
were and did during the 'Viking Age' (roughly the three hundred years
between the end of the eighth and eleventh centuries). In the English
popular imagination, for example, they are commonly supposed to be
the ones who do the most to fill the gap between the Romans leaving
in the fifth century and the Normans arriving in the eleventh, even
though it is the Anglo-Saxons who chronologically and geographically
have a much larger claim on filling this historical space. Visually speaking, the Vikings account for one of the most well-defined bodies of
medieval images, from horned helmets (alas, a modern misconception)
to longships (an image more securely anchored in medieval reality
thanks to some spectacular archaeological discoveries). The repertoire
of powerful and memorable images helps to explain why the Vikings
have influenced countless visions of the barbarian and his world, good
and bad, in fantasy-based books, films and games. It is significant that
J. R. R. Tolkien, author of the *Lord of the Rings* which has gained even
greater popularity since being made into three blockbuster movies, was
an expert on Anglo-Saxon literature, a body of material which includes
celebrations of heroic values (for example in the epic *Beowulf*, which is
actually set in Scandinavia) and of brave resistance against menacing
Viking invaders (such as in the *Battle of Maldon*, an account of a serious
Danish defeat of the English in 991). Far less pretentiously, but perhaps
just as influentially, in the 'Horrible Histories' series of popular history
books aimed at British children, one comes across *The Vicious Vikings*,
somewhere between *The Smashing Saxons* and *The Stormin' Normans*.

The Vikings have not always played such a starring role in the historical imagination. In Scandinavia itself, they were largely rediscovered
in the nineteenth and early twentieth centuries under the influence of
Romantic and nationalistic sentiment. In America, as we have seen, the

dominant Columbus-centred narrative of national origins militated against paying too much attention to the Norse adventures in the Atlantic (although, as the nineteenth century wore on, the pro-Viking lobby increased in size and assertiveness, due in part to the substantial Scandinavian migration to Canada and the United States, especially the Upper Midwest). In Britain, too, the Vikings were slow to enter the limelight. Take, for example, the work of Sir Walter Scott, who we have seen probably did more to popularize images of the Middle Ages than any other individual. Although Scott demonstrated a keen interest in some aspects of the Viking age, as revealed by his poem *Harold the Dauntless* (1817) and the novels *The Pirate* (1821) and *Count Robert of Paris* (1831), it is interesting that he missed a big trick in his most influential work, *Ivanhoe*. The plot of *Ivanhoe* turns on the conflict in twelfth-century England between the new political and social order represented by the Norman masters, and what survives of the old Anglo-Saxon world from the time before the Conquest. Although *Ivanhoe* is set in the reign of Richard I (1189–99), in other words more than a century after 1066, Scott uses a number of devices to collapse the chronology and so make the mid-eleventh century seem much closer and more relevant. The action all takes place in the East Midlands and Yorkshire, areas which had been significantly affected by Danish, that is, Viking, settlement in the ninth and tenth centuries. The Danes had a great impact on these areas' institutions, customs and (as we shall see in more detail in Chapter 4) language. But, one or two fleeting references aside, this vitally important factor in the ethnography of central medieval England does not register in *Ivanhoe* at all. Instead, we are offered a straightforward binary distinction between the Normans and the indigenous 'Saxons', whose Englishness swallows up any distinctive Danish contribution to the mix.

As the nineteenth century progressed, however, interest in the Viking age picked up in Britain and elsewhere, thanks in large part to the wider dissemination, translation and vulgarization of Norse literature, which is one of the most distinctive and engaging bodies of medieval vernacular writing. Between the twelfth and fourteenth centuries there was a remarkable flourishing of writing in Old Norse, especially by poets and historians living in Iceland. Iceland might seem like an odd place to be the home of a great literary tradition: discovered and settled by Scandinavians as late as the ninth century (some Irish monks would seem to have got there earlier), it was a remote, thinly populated and politically marginal part of the Scandinavian world. But its writers, working in prose and verse, enjoyed a cultural reputation out of all proportion to Iceland's geopolitical status. Some of their output was about their own contemporary world, and has accordingly been used by modern scholars as a vital source for medieval Iceland's social history, including the celebrated institution of the bloodfeud. But much of their work looked beyond Iceland to the northern world in general, and back in time to what we would understand as the Viking Age, as well as further back still to the myths of the pagan gods such as Odin and Thor. Nineteenth-century readers, therefore, were offered a rich conspectus of the Viking world fixed on a variety of times and places. What they found there was, of course, filtered through their own desires and prejudices. William Morris went to Iceland twice in the 1870s and thought that he had discovered the sort of society in touch with its medieval past that he found so lacking back home. For others, at a time when Britannia ruled the waves, it seemed perfectly reasonable to trace the origins of British maritime greatness back to the seafaring traditions supposedly brought to the country many centuries earlier by the Danes and Norwegians.

Jingoistic possibilities aside, however, the most important thing about the Norse literature was that it was very rich, which made people aware of the complexities of Viking society even as they were hunting for facile connections to the present day. The images of typical Viking heroes that emerged, therefore, could be quite nuanced and layered, either because a hero was presented in a saga or poem as a complex character with conflicting qualities, or because different characters were depicted representing a range of contrasting virtues and vices. Overall, however, the original Norse literature was, unsurprisingly, positive about the people and the societies that it described, with the result that the Victorian vision of the Vikings conformed to this generally upbeat assessment. The best Vikings, including the cast of remarkable women which features in Icelandic literature, became seen as embodiments of bravery, hardiness, resourcefulness, magnanimity, steadfastness, loyalty and adventurousness – in general terms, not unlike the attributes of a Scott-esque chivalric hero, but more independent in keeping with the supposedly less hierarchical and less rigid social patterns of the north, and physically toughened up by the harsh climate and rigours of seafaring. Even the violent looters and pillagers could be toned down into something more like loveable rogues up to their boisterous tricks.

With different voices came different visions. As academic history developed from the second half of the nineteenth century, it favoured sources that were closer in time than the Icelandic sagas and poems to the Viking themselves, albeit at the expense of cultural proximity. This meant shifting attention back to the chronicles and annals of some of the Vikings' victims in places like England, France and Ireland. These closely contemporary accounts of the Vikings' activities were written by monks and clerics, representatives of precisely the sorts of institutions that were most vulnerable to Viking raids because their church orna-ments and treasures made the best loot. The result was an image of the Vikings that stressed their pagan otherness, their barbarity and violence. Much of the modern stereotype of the wild Viking, raping and pillaging, goes straight back to these anguished evocations of dark forces that somehow appeared on the horizon, as if from nowhere, and brought devastation in their wake.

With the development of medieval archaeology from around the middle of the twentieth century, however, popular images of the Vikings were offered a new and complicating vision. In a well-worn phrase, the Vikings came to be seen as 'traders, not raiders'. This is a distinction which had a long pedigree, and one of the very first recorded Anglo-Saxon confrontations with the Vikings turned on the potential for confusion that it could cause. According to the tenth-century chronicler Aethelweard, embellishing a story that he found in his ninth-century source, when three Viking ships landed on the Dorset coast during the reign of King Beorhtric of Wessex (786–802), the king's local representative made the mistake of assuming that these might be merchants looking for a place in which to do business, and so he bound down to the beach to meet them. The mistake proved fatal. Whether or not this sorry story was true, the significant thing is that this early memory of the Anglo-Saxon encounter with the Vikings was bound up with the notion that there could be more to Viking seafaring than simple acts of aggression.

Modern archaeology has tended to confirm that the royal represen-tative, Beaduheard, was perhaps more unlucky than stupid, because the excavations at numerous important sites such as Hedeby in northern Germany and York in England, as well as the discovery of hoards of coins, now suggest that the Vikings were involved in complex networks of trade that embraced not just north-western Europe but also the Mediterranean, the Baltic region, down into the Russian interior and as far as the Muslim Middle East. Just as importantly, the excavations of major settlements run counter to the image of the Vikings as fleeting, smash-and-grab raiders or alien invaders. What emerges is a more complex, more 'domestic' vision of long-term communities of men, women and children, not just a handful of tough masculine types squeezed into a longship. In the rush to undo the crude Viking stereotype, however, it was perhaps inevitable that the 'traders, not raiders' motto would become overworked and used to summon up images of Viking society that were far too sanitized. In recent decades, therefore, scholars have been working towards a more subtle understanding of the Vikings which synthesizes the 'voices' represented by the different types of sources: 'traders *and* raiders, and a lot more besides' would now be a better, if less catchy, tag. How far this will alter popular conceptions remains to be seen. To judge, for example, from *The Vicious Vikings* in the 'Horrible Histories' series, we still seem to want our Vikings to be bloodthirsty, larger than life, robust and resourceful.

The various ways in which the Vikings have been imagined are a good demonstration of how the relationships between popular and scholarly visions of the medieval past are constantly shifting. This dynamic as much as anything makes it useful for anyone studying the medieval past to be aware of the role that the Middle Ages play in modern culture. In particular it is important to know something about the period between the late eighteenth and late nineteenth centuries when the Middle Ages were invented as a cultural phenomenon. The latest manifestations of our cultural engagement with all things medieval come and go in quick succession: a hit movie set in the Middle Ages that is currently playing in cinemas, for example, will soon go to DVD and recede into the general referential background. So rather than attempt to keep up with the bewilderingly rapid turnover of disposal pop-cultural consumables, it makes more sense to go back to their roots and ultimate sources of inspiration in nineteenth-century literature, art and architecture. Not that the Middle Ages were first invented in the nineteenth century, of course. They had already been reconstructed, fought over and judged for years. In seventeenth- and eighteenth-century England, to cite just one instance, lawyers and constitutionalists had used the Middle Ages as a prime battleground in their debates about the status of the monarchy, parliament and the common law. On the other hand, the century or so after the French Revolution was a particularly formative phase for medievalism, because it was in this period that a variegated but compelling repertoire of images and associations about the Middle Ages came into being. This repertoire was what was available to the general cultural mix by the late nineteenth and early twentieth centuries, at which critical point it became caught up in, and to a large extent frozen by, the explosion of mass communications, the spread of education, the growth of the entertainment industries, and the greater significance attached to all manifestations of popular culture.

Paradoxically perhaps, in an age of instantaneous communication and rapid change, where everything seems impermanent and volatile, this very volatility keeps drawing us back to what have become canonical visions of the Middle Ages, even though these visions were themselves forged in a period which in many other respects has come to epitomize the old-fashioned and quaint. The results are constructions of the Middle Ages which combine bits of the real thing with multiple layers of self-referential cultural overlay. When, for example, we are shown to our seat at a *Medieval Times* venue ('call 1-888-WEJOUST') by a wench in what passes for period costume, and as we tuck into our notionally medieval feast before watching a less than entirely convincing staging of a tournament, we are both witnessing and to some extent enacting a pastiche of a pastiche of a pastiche. That is to say, we become part of a cartoon-like caricature of images and ideas that have become familiar from contemporary films, television shows and games that are themselves recycling earlier Hollywood caricatures of a fictional world created by Walter Scott and his ilk. Sitting down at *Medieval Times* and watching the show is a good metaphor, in fact, for how we are all complicit in the creation of the pop-cultural Middle Ages by being the consumers of its products.

That said, it is important not to exaggerate the depth of the nineteenth century's fascination with the Middle Ages, and so by extension the power of its continuing influence over us today. Other slices of history, most noticeably ancient Egypt, were available to satisfy people's appetite for the exotic, and this appetite was further fed by Europe's imperial reach around the world. Not all writers and artists chose to jump on the medievalist bandwagon, or to stay on it very long if they did. For example, Robert Browning's *The Pied Piper of Hamelin* (1842) is the best known telling of this famous story set in the fourteenth century, but it was far from representative of Browning's output in general. He disliked what he saw as the corruption and superstition of the Middle Ages, and the medievalist vogue largely passed him by. The most ardent enthusiasms could sometimes cool: unlike William Morris, Victor Hugo did not carry his youthful medievalism with him as his politics moved to the left in later life; and even Scott himself wearied of the Middle Ages towards the end of his career when he was forced to crank out book after book in order to pay off enormous debts. For all the Victorian taste for paintings depicting medieval scenes, historical or literary, these were outnumbered by images of the post-medieval world; the seventeenth century was especially popular. And for every advocate of medieval art and architecture there were always other people defending the artistic and intellectual superiority of the classical world. The Middle Ages were just one element, then, within an eclectic mix of tastes, styles and enthusiasms, and this is the status that they have retained.

On the other hand, Scott's celebrity, the enormous sums invested in large Gothic buildings, and the artistic influence of the Pre-Raphaelites, to cite just three indicators, are hardly the signs of a minor fad. Nineteenth-century debates about the Middle Ages may have lost their political edge, but in other respects we still need to be aware of them. This is so for two reasons. In the first place, it helps us to be alive to the processes whereby we fashion our ideas about the medieval period. As we shall see in Chapter 3, the surviving sources on which we must base our understanding of the Middle Ages are very patchy and difficult to assess. There are not only many gaping holes in the evidence but also, and more insidiously, half-gaps which create as many problems of interpretation as they appear to resolve. In these circumstances, we are regularly required to draw on our imaginative resources – which is not, it must be stressed, the same as 'making things up' – in order to compensate for the large grey areas in our understanding. When we do this, we need to be particularly vigilant about the sources of our ideas. As we make assumptions about medieval people's interior selves and lived experiences in order to move our analysis from A to C when evidence for B is missing, can we be absolutely sure that these assumptions are validated by other pieces of genuinely medieval evidence? Or are we, unconsciously, slipping across into medievalism in order to retrieve the images and ideas that we need in order to make our argument work? Do we find ourselves attaching greater significance to those aspects of medieval civilization for which the pop-cultural 'coverage' is fullest, at the expense of those people and activities that feature less? Do we downgrade, for example, the poor compared to the rich, women compared to men, the drab and routine compared to the opulent and glamorous, and the world of intellectual effort compared to the overt and visually rich physicality of something like a tournament? An awareness of the medievalist legacy is an invaluable aid to the self-reflection that is a critical part of any effective study of the Middle Ages.

Second, thinking about medievalism is a good route into an appreciation of the complexity of the Middle Ages themselves. The point to stress here is that the pop-cultural clichés and stereotypes are not necessarily *wrong*. It is true that they are usually gross distortions of reality, they have to be highly selective in order to work, and they always over-simplify; but this is not the same as saying that the real Middle Ages amount to an equivalent but entirely opposite vision, like a photographic negative. Put another way, discovering about the medieval past does not normally involve turning a familiar image or association through a complete 180°, which would soon make the whole thing a mechanical exercise involving little or no imagination. More often than not the angle of deflection will be less, and calculating what it is becomes part of the intellectual challenge. As we shall see in the next chapter, one of the main traps into which someone studying the Middle Ages can fall is to make sweeping assumptions about medieval civilization across the board, when in fact it was immensely diverse. An appreciation of the liberties that popular culture takes with the Middle Ages, therefore, is a way of being forewarned and forearmed to be sceptical about all those other generalizations and truisms, the ones which seem to come with a scholarly stamp of approval, that we encounter in our reading.

2
What are the 'Middle Ages'?

In the late eleventh and early twelfth centuries, in the schools of northern France which were among the forerunners of the medieval university, one of the biggest intellectual debates to attract the attention of scholars was the relationship between words and things, and by extension the ways in which language does or does not capture the reality of the world that we perceive around us. This debate was no empty academic exercise. Perhaps the greatest thinker of the age, Peter Abelard, cut his intellectual teeth on the problem. At stake ultimately was the way in which people could say that they understood God, whose revelation to humankind was believed to be transmitted through the Bible, that is to say, through words. 'In the beginning was the Word, and the Word was with God, and the Word was God', as the opening of the Gospel of St John declares. Does something exist independently of our having a word for it, so that words are simply after-the-fact labels that we devise in order to describe the world to one another satisfactorily? Or does a word have a more active function, actually creating the notion of the thing that it designates? The issue was never fully resolved (though Abelard characteristically believed that he had managed it) and over the years it has continued to crop up in various guises, up to and including some of the debates generated by contemporary poststructuralism. For our purposes, it is an appropriate illustration from the medieval period itself of the basic problems that surround our use of the terms 'Middle Ages' and 'medieval'. Do these labels capture a reality that actually existed, or do they force one version of reality on us at the expense of other, unvoiced, possibilities?

Periodization is an inescapable part of the study of history at all levels. It involves two related processes. First, we slice up the past into pieces of varying sizes, and then we allocate special names, labels that help us to demarcate each slice as something distinct and unique. Periodization is embedded in the structure of school and university syllabuses, the titles of academic organizations, even job titles. We like to think that we can rise above the constraints of periodization, but no individual can hope to gain an in-depth knowledge of anything more than a tiny fraction of the totality of human experience, and so slicing history up into manageable portions makes studying the past a more focused, realistic and ultimately exciting prospect. To this extent, at least, periodization serves a positive end. On the other hand, the ways in which historians divide the past up into workable pieces have evolved in a very haphazard manner over many centuries, with the result that there is no coherent system that works equally well for all periods and all parts of the world. The problem is compounded by the fact that we use a wide variety of labels. Some are very old and hallowed by tradition irrespective of their actual validity; we shall see later that 'medieval' falls into this category. Others labels are expressions of recent trends in historical scholarship, but the problem here is that academic trends come and go, and few things date more quickly than the latest fashion. The obvious solution would be to switch the labels that are applied to the past as each new historiographical vogue comes along. But the snag then becomes that the terminology that fashion-conscious scholars devise can easily descend into an in-house code only understood by a minority of specialists in the know, something which is likely to confuse and alienate people coming to the subject from outside. At the other extreme, however, scholarly awareness of this potential problem can sometimes translate into a reluctance to jettison old labels which have clearly outlived any usefulness that they may once have possessed.

Even the most innocent-looking historical labels are never entirely neutral. The Middle Ages are a case in point. On the surface the term is simply a relational one that situates one period in between two others. Our word 'medieval' ultimately derives from the Latin *medium* = middle + *aevum* = era/age. It all looks very straightforward. But, as we shall see, it is impossible to place one fenced-off, labelled piece of time between two others without asking *why* you are doing it, and the answers to this question, even if only implicitly, will always be embedded in the terminology that comes to be applied. We have seen in Chapter 1 how the Middle Ages are a magnet for stereotypes and misconceptions in the realm of popular culture, but something broadly similar can also be true of academic discourse. Whenever historians use a historical label, they are giving it a stamp of authority and legitimacy. The label thereby becomes a form of shorthand for the values that are associated with a particular period, as well as for the methodological approaches, substantive issues and intellectual debates that historians emphasize in order to animate discussion of their chosen piece of the past.

One way to limit the amount of baggage that a historical label can carry is to use terms which were not current at the time. The further back in time one goes, of course, the easier it becomes to introduce an element of terminological detachment as the languages that people used and their basic conceptual frameworks become more and more unlike our own. The terms 'Middle Ages' and 'medieval' are good in this respect because, obviously, they were not used in the Middle Ages themselves. If one draws on terms that were in use during the period one is studying, there is a real danger of taking people at their own estimation. An excellent example of this problem, which also has a close bearing on our understanding of 'medieval', is the use of the term 'Renaissance' in relation to changes in European civilization between about 1300 and 1600. The origins of this label lie in the language of rebirth and renovation that was used by fourteenth- and fifteenth-century intellectuals in central and northern Italy, especially in and around Florence, to describe contemporary trends in art, architecture and literature in terms of a return to the civilization of ancient Rome. The term was picked up in the nineteenth century by the influential and popular French historian Jules Michelet, and it then received its most influential endorsement in the ground-breaking work of the Swiss scholar Jacob Burckhardt, whose *The Civilization of the Renaissance in Italy* appeared in 1860.

Since Burckhardt the subject has expanded enormously, and with this have come new questions of definition. Is the Renaissance best seen as a historical period or as a movement? Is it limited to elite culture, or does the term have wider applications, so that one may speak, for example, of 'Renaissance monarchy'? Was there a single point of origin, fourteenth- and fifteenth-century Florence, or are we dealing with scattered clusters of diverse phenomena? Did the Renaissance 'happen' at different times in different places, for example in northern Europe later than in Italy? Did northern Europe have a Renaissance at all? Did the chronology of change vary for different forms of cultural expression such as architecture, poetry and music? Did women experience the Renaissance in the same ways as men? Overall, did Renaissance thinkers overestimate their closeness to classical antiquity and underestimate their debt to late medieval culture? The effect of these and many other questions has been to blur the boundaries between medieval and Renaissance culture and to move attention away from the old certainties that flowed from Burkhardt's confidence that the Renaissance's image of itself was a indeed a fair representation of the underlying reality. This is all to the good. But the term 'Renaissance' itself is very resilient, not only in the popular consciousness but also in some scholarly circles; there are many Renaissance specialists in a range of disciplines who are uncomfortable at the thought of being rebranded early modernists or even late medievalists. As long as the concept persists, it means that any discussion of the subject that draws on it will always, by one route or another, find itself returning to the question of how much a term coined more than 600 years ago remains valid as a category of modern analysis. This is a perfectly interesting question in and of itself, but it seems a rather slender basis on which to build the comparative study of a tremendously vast, complex, variegated and thematically rich body of cultural material, some of which is indeed different and innovative compared to what we normally associate with the Middle Ages, but some of which is demonstrably a seamless continuation of late medieval civilization.

By simple virtue of its being a post-medieval invention, then, the word 'medieval' introduces a valuable element of objectivity and distance. But this is more than offset by the many negative associations that the term has accumulated since it was invented. The origins of the idea of a middle period are to be found in the writings of Renaissance intellectuals in the fourteenth and fifteenth centuries. Perhaps the most influential was the writer Petrarch (1304–74), who is often credited with putting the darkness into the 'Dark Ages'. By the fifteenth century writers in Florence and elsewhere were beginning to talk of a 'middle era' (in Latin *media tempestas* or *media tempora*), and the prestige of avant-garde Italian ideas ensured that this notion would carry over into other parts of Europe. At this stage, the identification of a middle period was not an attempt at the sort of all-inclusive historical periodization that we often apply today. The focus of these early commentators and theorists was on high-status artistic productions, and the criteria on which they based their judgements were essentially aesthetic. In his influential *On Painting* (c.1435), for example, Leon Battista Alberti bemoaned the loss of the skills that had been practised in 'our most vigorous antique past', and set about trying to revive them for his contemporaries.

Another excellent illustration of this approach to the past is to be found in *The Lives of the Most Eminent Painters, Sculptors and Architects* published by Giorgio Vasari in 1550 (an expanded version appeared in 1568). Writing after 200 years of Renaissance thought and artistic effort, Vasari was attempting to build on the perspectives of writers such as Alberti by pulling together the lives of different artists into one explanatory framework. He hoped that this would create a single, coherent story of art's rise, fall, and rebirth. Tracing the emergence of art from the Creation to the ancient civilizations such as Babylon, Egypt, Israel, and especially Greece and Rome, Vasari argued that artistic standards had begun to decline in the late Roman period. The triumphal arch erected in Rome in the early fourth century AD, to mark the defeat in 312 of the main rival of the emperor Constantine (306–37), was, Vasari argued, emblematic of this deterioration. When the Germanic invaders and the Huns destroyed the Roman empire in the West, the arts went into further steep decline as brutish baseness replaced civilized sophistication as the culture of the ruling elites. Artistic production became inept, misshapen, vile and barbarous. There were some glimmers of hope in architecture from the tenth and eleventh centuries onwards, as a few pioneers began to copy old Roman designs, but it was only from the middle of the thirteenth century that 'the rudeness of the modern use' in architecture was overcome, and people also began to aspire to the standards set by ancient sculptors and painters. The key pioneers of this rebirth included the artists Cimabue (d.1300) and Giotto (d.1337). Subsequent generations then built on their achievements, so that for Vasari the pinnacle had been reached with the work of Leonardo da Vinci (1452–1519) and 'the divine Michelangelo' (1475–1564), significantly the two Renaissance names that are most fixed in the popular consciousness even today.

On one level this looks like the myth-making of a tiny elite of artists, patrons and critics, which is precisely what it was, but the sort of aesthetic judgements formed by people such as Alberti and Vasari had a wider resonance. In the first place, the various movements in thought and practice that we (unsatisfactorily) group together under the term 'Renaissance' extended beyond art, architecture and sculpture to include poetry, music, history-writing, science, language-teaching, philosophy, political thought and many other branches of learning. These changes were mostly evident at the elite end of the cultural spectrum, of course, but their cumulative effect was to create a sense of profound detachment from the past among the most influential sections of society. This reinforced the sense that the barbarism of the 'middle period' was a general phenomenon applying to intellectual, artistic and cultural life across the board, not just to certain manifestations of it. Secondly, and following on from this perspective, it was natural for elite writers and their readers, when thinking about the arts, to suppose that what we would call a society's 'high culture' was the most important and interesting manifestation of any given time and place in history. What might begin as an aesthetic judgement applied to one or two artistic forms, therefore, could expand progressively to become an assessment of the fundamental characteristics of a whole historical civilization. Thus, by the sixteenth and seventeenth centuries, scholars and intellectuals were beginning to think in terms of the 'middle age' as a global periodization applying to the political and religious as well as the cultural history of post-Roman Europe. It is sometimes said that the term 'Middle Ages' was definitively coined by a Swedish scholar named Christoph Keller (also known as Cellarius) in his *Historia Medii Aevi* (History of the Middle Ages), which appeared in 1688, but his claim to fame as the inventor of the idea is exaggerated, for the notion of a discrete historical period and form of civilization in the interval between ancient Rome and the Renaissance had already taken firm root by his day.

On the other hand, there still was, and long remained, considerable room for doubt about when this middle period began and ended. Perhaps the Middle Ages as we know them now were only truly invented in the nineteenth century, when some of the ideas and associations that had been swirling around for centuries were worked into a clearer and more rigid scheme that satisfied contemporary tastes for ordered, 'scientific' history. The single most important development in this context was the creation in Germany soon after the end of the Napoleonic Wars of the *Gesellschaft für Deutschlands ältere Geschichtskunde* (the Society for the Study of Early German History), the aim of which was to produce high-quality editions of medieval sources such as chronicles, charters, laws and letters. This project set new standards of technical proficiency, and the series of works that it began, the *Monumenta Germaniae Historica*, or Germany's Historical Monuments (i.e. sources), is still going strong. Soon after the Society was first formed in 1819, its founding fathers decided to set terminal dates of 500 and 1500 for its work. In practice, these cut-off points were never observed rigidly, but the huge prestige that the *Monumenta* enjoyed in academic circles helped to cement its version of the chronological limits of the Middle Ages. This was reinforced by the fact that its understanding of what constituted 'German' blurred into what we would call 'Germanic', with the result that the early medieval histories of places such as France, Italy, and Spain also fell within its remit. This broad vision was the one carried over when the modern-style teaching of history began to emerge in schools and universities in the second half of the nineteenth century, becoming enshrined in the creation of new syllabuses and new academic titles. This system is essentially what universities today have inherited.

The years 500 and 1500 have a neat look to them, but in practice it has always proved possible to do some fiddling around the edges provided the basic chronological scheme is respected. In different countries, different terminal dates have commended themselves as reflections of the different narratives of national history. In Britain (and more specifically England), for example, it used to be common to end the Middle Ages in 1485, the year in which the last Plantagenet king, Richard III, was defeated at Bosworth by the future Henry VII, the founder of the Tudor dynasty. A great deal of modern scholarship has been devoted to establishing the many continuities that can be found in politics and government across the traditional divide, or to arguing that if there were key transitions, they happened earlier or later. Nonetheless 1485 lives on in the popular consciousness to some extent, and it also remains convenient scholarly shorthand for the medieval-to-modern break. Similarly, in France there is a long tradition of starting the Middle Ages in 496, the year in which, so it is believed, the Frankish king Clovis was baptized. Recent research is showing that the date is probably wrong, and that in any event Clovis' 'conversion' was actually a shift to Catholicism from another form of Christianity, not an epoch-making movement from pagan (= ancient) to Christian (= medieval) belief. Nonetheless the year still matters as a potent symbol, as demonstrated by the exhibitions and public commemorations organized for the fifteen hundredth anniversary in 1996.

Other dates have been chosen because their significance applies to Europe as a whole. This is the basis of the two most common terminal dates: 476, the year in which the last Roman emperor in the West was deposed (though in fact there was another imperial contender up to 480, and one must not forget that the sequence of emperors continued in the eastern part of the Empire up to 1453); and 1492, the year in which Christopher Columbus set out on his first voyage across the Atlantic and reached the Caribbean islands (though when one reads his account of the journey one is struck by the oddly low-key way in which it treats the 'first contact' encounter with the local people, an event which we nowadays imagine must have been one of the most charged moments in history). Historians often dislike fixed terminal dates because it seems to favour a rather old-fashioned view of history as a series of important events (or *histoire événementielle*, to borrow a useful

French term). There is a great deal to be said for this wariness, especially because event-centred history tends to elevate politics and warfare above other facets of human experience, such as, say, population change or environmental history, which are necessarily tracked across long stretches of time and cannot be pinned down to single defining moments. On the other hand, dates can be useful if they are used carefully as markers for long-term processes, not just one-off events viewed in isolation. 476 looks back to what once was, 1492 looks forward to what will be. They are the dates of supposedly momentous events, but they can also stand emblematically for processes that played out over much longer periods. This double-edged quality makes them work pretty well as clean boundaries that mark an intervening middle period.

Dates, then, can work as dividers provided one remembers that they only have a symbolic value and do not somehow 'prove' that significant historical change always happens abruptly. The problem then becomes, however, how to decide between the competing merits of different symbols. If not 476, then why not 312, the year in which the Roman emperor Constantine acknowledged Christianity; 325, the date of the Council of Nicaea, where Constantine's presence at a gathering of the senior clergy neatly symbolizes the very close relationship between the Church and secular government that was to characterize the medieval West as well as East; 363, the date of the death of the last pagan emperor, Julian; the Visigoth sack of Rome in 410 (or the Vandal sack of Rome in 455); the death in 454 of Aetius, the last effective Roman military leader in the West; the execution in 523 of the philosopher Boethius, a member of the old Roman aristocracy that had collaborated with the new Germanic regime in Italy; 535, the start of the hugely destructive attempt by the emperor in Constantinople, Justinian (527–65), to reconquer Italy for the Empire; or 630, the year in which the emperor Heraclius entered in triumph into Jerusalem to celebrate his recent against-the-odds victory over Sassanian Persia, the latest manifestation, that is to say, of the civilization to the east of the Mediterranean that had for many centuries fuelled first the Greeks' and then the Romans' sense of the 'Other'? These examples could be multiplied many times over, and the same is true of the other end of the Middle Ages. If not 1492, why not 1453, the fall of Constantinople to the Ottoman Turks? Or 1494, the year of the invasion of Italy by the armies of the French king, which can be construed as the dawn of a new phase in European power-politics? Or 1517, when Martin Luther nailed his 95 theses to the church door at Wittenberg, an event that has come to symbolize the beginning of the Reformation? Or 1521, when

Hernán Cortés and his conquistadors (as well as, it should be stressed, many local allies) finally smashed the power of the Aztec empire in Mexico? Or 1527, the sack of Rome by the armies of the emperor Charles V?

An interesting effect of playing this game of dates is that it becomes difficult, if not downright impossible, to elevate the claims of one date to particular symbolic significance without having to acknowledge the potential merits of many others. Ultimately, therefore, the process proves self-defeating. More significantly still, if one applies a range of criteria drawn from different branches of history – political, religious, military, scientific and others – in order to come up with clusters of potentially significant dates for the beginning and end of the Middle Ages, then it begins to look very strange that these clusters should be most conspicuous either side of c.500 and c.1500, give or take a century or so, and not in the very long expanse of time that falls in between. If one subjects this intermediate period to the same exercise, however, one quickly comes up with a long list of symbolically charged dates. But if that is so, why must *all* of these be less significant than *all* of our original examples? In other words, reducing signpost dates to the role of symbols, which is all they are, exposes how arbitrary it is to privilege two periods or phases – the years around 500 and those around 1500 – as necessarily and intrinsically more meaningful than anything that happened in the intervening thousand years.

It could be objected that historians seldom use single dates as key parts of their analyses, and that they argue instead in terms of long periods of transition. This is perfectly true and is an excellent illustration of the methodological deepening and thematic broadening of historical research over the last few decades. A great deal of recent research has shown, for example, that the Roman Empire in the West did not so much 'fall' as dissolve over the course of many centuries. One illustration of the need to track change over the long term is the fact that many of the fundamental problems that beset the late Roman state and played a significant part in its eventual demise, such as difficulties in recruiting and supplying its armies and in raising the taxes to plough into military organization, go back at least as early as the third century. Similarly, a famous thesis formulated by the pioneering economic historian Henri Pirenne (1862–1935) argued that the basic economic system of the late Roman world survived the political collapse of the western empire in the fifth century because the Mediterranean remained a Roman 'lake' binding together the societies around it through trade and other links. This connection was only broken with the emergence of Islam in the seventh century. As the Arabs made spectacular military conquests along the north African coast and into the Roman Middle East, they shattered the unity of this economic and cultural zone. This meant that the societies of north-western Europe, now economically cut off and thrown onto their own resources, had to develop new forms of wealth-creation based on the exploitation of land and on small-scale, local markets; and it was these new forms which were the basic underpinning of what became medieval society. Hence Pirenne's famous aphorism that without Mohammed, the founder of Islam, Charlemagne, the king of the Franks between 768 and 814, the first western ruler since the fifth century to revive the title of emperor, and the model *par excellence* for many later generations of rulers, would have been impossible. This thesis has been much debated and modified, not least because of enormous advances in archaeology since Pirenne's day, but for our purposes it is a good illustration of the value of thinking about long-term shifts in society and culture, rather than looking for the sudden and momentous event even when single events themselves, such as the military victories of the Arab armies, form part of the bigger picture.

The particular value of this sort of approach is that it allows for different sorts of transitions, political, economic, cultural, technological, environmental, and demographic, to be happening at the same time, and thereby better reflects the enormous complexity of human social experience. It also allows for changes to occur at different rates, and with different outcomes, in different places. This is vitally important because arguments for sudden change often proceed on the basis of privileging the perspectives of a small section of society, usually a rich, adult, male, educated elite positioned in the political centre, whereas other types of people in other situations would have experienced the forces shaping their lives in different ways. On the other hand, an emphasis on transitions rather than single dates only fudges the essential problem rather than solves it. For, if we still persist with the same basic binary divisions, classical-medieval and medieval-early modern/Renaissance, then this creates the expectation that at each end of the medieval period there was one decisive type of transition, the Big One, which was more significant than, and ultimately exercised a unique determining influence on, all the others. Whether you like your boundaries crisp or smudgy ultimately makes no difference as long as you believe that there is a real boundary out there somewhere waiting to be found.

If we stop focusing on the existence of boundaries in the first place, then the notion of the 'Middle Ages' is exposed as entirely artificial. This can be further demonstrated by looking at how our sense of what made medieval life medieval is subtly but significantly inflected by the knock-on effects of the terminology we use for the period that comes next. If we think in terms of 'early modern history', this can subsume a wide range of historical changes. These might include a growth in the power and resources of national governments, which we can now begin to call 'states' without fear of anachronism; the growth of moveable-type printing; the extension of European maritime activity eastwards to Asia and westwards to the New World; the Protestant Reformation and the Catholic Counter-Reformation. If we think in terms of the 'Renaissance', however, we are narrowing the focus to single out intellectual and artistic trends. These two clearly overlap. It would be impossible, for instance, to think about changes in Renaissance painting without considering the courtly culture and political self-fashioning of the rulers who patronized artists. But there are subtle differences. 'Early modern' is a potentially all-inclusive term whereas 'Renaissance' is more limited in its associations because it is mostly concerned with elite culture, as well as being more obviously gendered in its implications: as Joan Kelly asked in a famous article, 'Did women have a Renaissance?' The point here is that something as seemingly innocuous as a preference for one label or another has a substantial retroactive effect on our sense of what it is about the Middle Ages that mattered most. What, in other words, gives the Middle Ages their precise 'exit velocity'?

There are many other problems with our continuing attachment to the 'Middle Ages' and 'medieval'. One is the enormous chronological distortion that it introduces. Even if we accept the word 'medieval' as it has come to be used, the middle-ness that it expresses is coming to appear more and more inappropriate. The word worked well enough in its own terms in the days when the period before the Middle Ages was understood very narrowly to mean the thousand years or so between about 500 BC and 500 AD, and was geographically focused on Greece and Rome, with perhaps some extensions further back into ancient Egypt and Assyria, and the Israel of the Old Testament. Archaeology in particular has enormously expanded our knowledge of the chronological depth and geographical range of the ancient world, and this has pushed back the boundaries of what was once consigned to 'prehistory'. The result of this expansion of our knowledge of the ancient world is that it forces the supposedly middle period that comes after it more and more off centre. Increasingly, then, the middle-ness of the Middle Ages seems to be based on a narrow and dated vision of what matters in world history.

A further problem flows on from this. The word 'medieval' enshrines a vision of human history that is squarely centred on European civilization, more specifically Western, Christian civilization, which is seen as the cradle of various forces for human progress. In recent decades historians have grown increasingly uncomfortable with any narrative of human history that relies on the notion of progress and privileges one part of the world by downgrading the importance of others. The old approach, it is argued, severely misrepresents the significance, and different chronologies, of civilizations in Asia, Africa and America. More than this, it limits our attention unreasonably to supposedly advanced civilizations rather than all the forms of human economic, political and social organization in their immense variety. 'Medieval', then, is accused of being too weighed down by its Eurocentric baggage to remain a useful or appropriate term. In this context, it is all the more curious that the word has found a new lease of life among some historians of places such as Africa and India, who use it to refer to the period before the age of Western colonialism. The residual influence of Marxist thought has something to do with this, with its vision of societies passing through different developmental phases characterized by the ways in which wealth is generated and which elements in society get to control it. In this vision, 'medieval' is effectively a synonym for 'feudal' as shorthand for one of these phases, the one marked out by the dominance of a land-owning aristocracy whose wealth derives from their exploitation of a dependent peasantry. The effect of this borrowing is unfortunate, because the historians of these places might think that they are using 'medieval' as another, fairly neutral, way of saying 'pre-colonial', 'pre-modern' or 'pre-industrial', while they are in fact, and not always consciously, forcing the reader into inappropriate and contrived comparisons with European history. In fact, the value of the word 'medieval' can only stand or fall on the basis of its applicability to a certain expanse of time in western European history: the time and place, that is to say, for which the term was invented in the first place. Anything else is downright misplaced.

Terms can be so loaded that it becomes almost impossible to apply them as historical labels without reinforcing their false assumptions about the internal coherence of what they purport to designate. A good example of this is the use of the term 'the Sixties' to denote something more loaded with meaning than a straightforward ten-year slice of time. As the poet Philip Larkin famously wrote in his *Annus Mirabilis*, sexual intercourse (and so by extension the whole sexual and cultural revolution of the Sixties) started in 1963, between the lifting of the ban on D. H. Lawrence's *Lady Chatterley's Lover* and the release of the Beatles' first LP. The chronology does not in fact stand up to close scrutiny: the landmark trial in which the publishers of *Lady Chatterley's Lover* were unsuccessfully prosecuted for obscenity took place in October–November 1960; and the album *Please Please Me* came out in Britain in March 1963. But Larkin's use of poetic licence nicely demonstrates the point that a date such as 1963, and the era which it supposedly opens, can take on an emblematic significance which transcends what actually happened. Any appreciation of the 'Sixties' conceived in the same sorts of ways that Larkin envisaged, as a distinctive social, cultural and political moment, would, moreover, need to extend into the 1970s, up to the Oil Crisis in 1973, for example, or the American withdrawal from Vietnam.

In general terms, the 'Sixties' evokes various more or less concurrent movements in parts of the Western world involving music and other facets of pop culture, shifts in gender politics, social liberalization, and civil rights reform. Processes such as the Vietnam War and the opposition it provoked (but not, significantly, the support it received) have become condensed into a gallery of iconic images that, we can be made to believe, capture the look and feel of this period. A good way of thinking about this is to consider how often we see shows on television which evoke the Sixties by flashing up a small but powerful repertoire of cliched images: for example, the flickering footage of the assassination of President John F. Kennedy, the Beatles arriving in New York, Martin Luther King giving a speech, hippies out of their heads (or mugging for the camera?) at Haight-Ashbury during the Summer of Love, Huey helicopters flying low over paddyfields, all this set to a soundtrack of The Rolling Stones' 'Paint it Black' or the organ solo in The Doors' 'Light My Fire'. The more we encounter this sort of selection of evocative images and sounds, and the more we practise joining up the dots to fill in what is left unstated, the more validated the 'Sixties' becomes as a point of historical reference, and the more we trust that there is indeed a master-narrative which draws all the disparate elements together. In reality, of course, there are many powerful reasons for challenging the portmanteau use of the term. The cultural and social changes associated with the Sixties affected different parts of the world, even different parts of the West, in diverse ways. And perceptions of what was happening varied according to age, class, educational background and gender. There was no single 'Sixties' at all. Nonetheless, the term creates an expectation, and we find ourselves trying to meet it. Precisely the same thing happens whenever we use 'Middle Ages' or 'medieval'.

At least the 'Sixties' only lasted a decade or so, and if people choose to take different positions on when they began and ended, the disagreements are only going to turn on a few years either way. By and large, the slices into which we divide history become shorter and more precisely delineated the nearer we get to the present day. Think, for example, of the range of subtle but significant differences that can be evoked by juxtaposing the 'Sixties' against the 'Fifties' or the 'Seventies'. The further back in time we go, however, the thicker the slicing. We can imagine, for instance, *belles époques, fins de siècles*, Golden Ages, *anciens régimes*, and so forth that lasted anything from a few decades to a century or so. By the time that we get back to around 1500, the coarsening process has reached the point where we can happily countenance a block of history lasting a thousand years. Why? Because not much changed during that time. And why did not much change? Because it was the Middle Ages. The circularity of the argument is obvious, but the assumptions that underpin it are nonetheless powerful. Even the subdivision of the Middle Ages into different phases – 'early'/'central'/'late' or 'early'/'high', for example – only reinforces the problem by trying to identify subtle shades of difference while implicitly validating the overall category of medieval-ness.

The basic problem is the sheer chronological and geographical mass of what normally falls under the heading 'medieval'. If the lived experiences of a seventh-century Italian aristocrat, a tenth-century German nun, a twelfth-century Spanish bishop and a fourteenth-century Icelandic farmer are all in some way 'medieval', what are we saying? That despite all the numerous and profound differences that separate these individuals' mental and physical worlds, there must nonetheless be something deep, deep down in a fundamental, perhaps unsensed, recess of their being which they all have in common. And secondly, we are saying that it is thanks to this shared quality that we are equipped to speak of their common medieval-ness. But what on earth could this mysterious essence be? And if it is such a fundamental part of these people's beings, which logically it has to be to include every man, woman and child in half a continent over a millennium, then how strange that this same essence should be wholly and abruptly absent from the people on either side of the traditional cut-off points, from, say, a third-century Roman prostitute or a sixteenth-century Protestant preacher. This is an obvious point, of course, but one that needs to be made: 'medieval' is simply too unwieldy.

This exposes another problem, that of asymmetry within and at either end of a historical period. The longer the period that a label covers, the more glaring this problem appears. Take, for example, the 'Sixties' as previously discussed. Whatever particular nuance we might place on our chosen definition of the term, by emphasizing political and economic conditions, for example, or pop-cultural trends, it is a fairly straightforward exercise to begin and end the period by applying the same sets of criteria. To take a superficial but clear example: if the Sixties started around the time of the Beatles' first LP, then perhaps they ended when the Beatles broke up in 1970. Whatever our chosen dates and the route we take to arrive at them, we are equipped to apply a label such as the 'Sixties' to the extent that we are tracking the emergence and then disappearance of selected diagnostic characteristics which we believe had an unbroken existence in the intervening period. The intro and the outro are in some sort of balance. To take another example, we might argue that the term 'Golden Age' when used of the seventeenth-century Dutch Republic is justified by the emergence, continuing presence and then decline or disappearance of a number of key features such as commercial prosperity, political expansion and artistic accomplishment. The period lasts longer than the decade or so covered by the 'Sixties', but it is still reasonably tightly delineable, with the result that the changes in conditions that mark its beginning and end stand in some sort of equal-and-opposite relationship to one another.

But when one comes to a period as large and unwieldy as the Middle Ages, any hope of symmetry vanishes. The problem is compounded by the fact that scholarly debates about the beginning and the end of the Middle Ages are seldom conducted with close and direct reference to each other. This is fair enough, because the two sets of scholars involved have specialisms about a thousand years apart. But the effect for the medievalist somewhere in the middle is like trying to listen to two different conversations at the same time. If, for the sake of argument, one were to say that the single most important transition from the classical to the medieval world was a social and economic transformation affecting the ways in which the land-owning minority exploited the human resources of the majority who worked the fields, then we would need to find an equivalent transition of equal significance to mark the end of the Middle Ages, if we want to balance things out. But if, again for the sake of argument, we were to consider that the most significant shift from the medieval to early modern worlds was cultural, a process primarily manifested in art, architecture and literature, then we present ourselves with a Middle Ages which seems to start one way and finish in quite another. Of course, both the socio-economic *and* cultural conditions of western Europe were very different in c.500 from what they were c.1500. But that is precisely the point: if there is so much difference at either end of the Middle Ages, why the need to use these particular times to frame a historical period in the first place?

The good news is that we are perhaps not so stuck with the terms 'medieval' and 'Middle Ages' as we might think. It is indeed possible to reduce, if not entirely eliminate, our dependency on addictive labels. The recent fate of the words 'feudal' and 'feudalism' offers an apt and salutary illustration. Strictly speaking, 'feudal' is the adjective relating to the noun 'fee' or 'fief'. A fief was what in modern legal parlance would be called the consideration of a contract: the material benefit or payment granted to someone when he (or, more rarely, she) entered into someone else's service and formally swore fidelity to him (or, more rarely, her). Often the fief consisted of one or more parcels of land, but it could be any income-generating source such as a share in a rent or a toll. In the classic textbook model of feudalism, the service promised to the lord was military in nature, especially what could be offered by a man equipped to fight as a knight or to lead a team of knights, but again there was a wide variety of arrangements according to the needs and status of the contracting parties. In narrow terms, therefore, feudal relationships operated on the level of what we would today call property law and the law of contract.

In practice, however, because earlier generations of historians believed that fief-holding was a fundamental feature of medieval life, especially between the eighth and thirteenth centuries, the range of associations connected to the words 'feudal' and 'feudalism' expanded to cover the whole political, military, economic, social and cultural environment in which the granting of fiefs took place. In the process, 'feudal society' became conceptualized not just as the time and place where fiefs happened to exist, but as a whole civilization characterized by, for example, the weakness of central governmental authority and the usurpation of power by local strongmen; the privatization of justice and law courts; the dominance of an aristocracy that emphasized its military identity in its self-fashioning; the exploitation by the aristocracy of the majority of the population, who were tied to the land by various legal and economic constraints; and particular institutional forms of that exploitation designed to facilitate group farming activity, for example in manors. The most influential exposition of 'feudal society' conceived in this broad sense was in the French historian Marc Bloch's *La société féodale*, which appeared in 1940 (an English translation, *Feudal Society*, was published in 1961). Bloch was the greatest medieval historian of his generation, perhaps the greatest ever, and his book can still be read with profit today even though most of its bigger arguments and many of its smaller ones have been overturned by more recent research.

Bloch's enormous influence placed a scholarly imprimatur on a maximal, all-inclusive reading of 'feudal' and 'feudalism'. This reinforced other, more overtly negative, approaches to the terms which had been gaining ground since the eighteenth and nineteenth centuries. One of the priorities of the French Revolution, for example, was to abolish the 'feudal' rights of the hated aristocracy. These were tax exemptions and legal privileges which mostly went back no further than 200 or so years. But it is easy to see how the rhetoric could be stretched further back in time to condemn the medieval predecessors (and in some cases distant ancestors) of the *ancien régime* aristocracy, an elite that had likewise prospered at the expense of the majority. In the nineteenth and twentieth centuries, under the influence of Marxist thought, feudalism became bound up with what was believed to be the period in human development before the advent of bourgeois capitalism; the main characteristics of this phase were thought to be the ascendancy of a largely rural aristocracy whose control of the means of production, essentially landed property and agricultural labour, was achieved through political and military mastery and the use of ties of dependency to keep the peasantry firmly in its place.

In these circumstances, it is not surprising that 'feudal' expanded to the point where it became a synonym for 'medieval' itself. A wonderful illustration of the ease with which the connection could be made comes from a film review written by the novelist Graham Greene in 1937. Greene was reviewing *Marked Woman*, a movie starring among others Bette Davis and an up-and-coming Humphrey Bogart. The film is set in a dark, seedy, criminal underworld. Greene wrote:

> 'It's feudal,' a character remarks with resignation in *Marked Woman*, and there are moments of creative imagination...in this picture of the night-club racket and the night-club baron which do convey some of the horror and pathos the Anglo-Saxon chronicler recorded of Stephen's reign: the exactions, the beatings and murders, and above all the hopelessness...It's been done before, of course, this picture of the feudal hell, but it has never been done better than in some of these scenes.[12]

This evocation of a feudal nightmare world is all the more fascinating for being based on an above-average knowledge of the Middle Ages.

The reference to the chronicler is to a well-known passage in one version of the *Anglo-Saxon Chronicle* which bemoans the disorder that had befallen England during the reign of King Stephen (1135–54), nineteen long years, it says, during which Christ and his saints slept. Given how much Greene warmed to his medieval theme, it seems almost churlish to point out that it was all a silly mistake. What the character in the film is actually saying is 'It's futile'. In fairness to Greene, the difference between the American pronunciations of 'futile' and 'feudal', which is clear enough to an American speaker, is usually lost on a British listener, who distinguishes differently between the sounds of 't' and 'd' placed between vowels, and rhymes 'futile' with 'mile'. For our purposes, the point to stress is the ease with which Greene, once he made the initial mistake, and pitching his remarks to a fairly broad readership, could mine a rich seam of associations and images, all of them dark, about medieval life in general.

Greene's usage still survives, in particular in relation to some of the more disapproving visions of medieval civilization that we encountered in Chapter 1. One sometimes encounters 'feudal' used in newspapers, for example, to describe the way of life in socially stratified, politically volatile and economically undeveloped parts of the Third World. Indeed, the word has survived as a means of registering disapproval of non-Western societies, and of affirming the idea of 'progress' towards Western-style liberal capitalism, without appearing to stray into political incorrectness. On the other hand, it is fair to say that the extent to which 'feudal' and 'feudalism' are current in popular discourses has declined in recent decades. In part this is because the appeal of Marxist thought has diminished since the end of the Cold War. But it also relates to changes in scholarly usage, and this is indeed one of the fairly rare examples of how historiographical fashions can alter popular perceptions in a fairly short space of time, if only negatively by cutting off the scholarly oxygen to a term or concept that has entered non-academic discourse. Medievalists today are generally much more wary of the terms 'feudal' and 'feudalism', and many try to avoid them altogether. A landmark event was the appearance in 1974 of an article by E. A. R. Brown, 'The Tyranny of a Construct: Feudalism and Historians of Medieval Europe'. In this article, Brown forcefully attacked the prevalence of the terms 'feudal' and 'feudalism' in academic debate. There were too many definitions in circulation to make the words useful, she pointed out, and every definition was so hedged around with geographical and chronological qualifications that even more confusion was the inevitable result. Moreover, the notion of the 'feudal system' was in fact a creation of lawyers and political theorists in the seventeenth and eighteenth centuries, not a true encapsulation of medieval conditions. Brown's article has been hugely influential, and rightly so. One way to judge this is to read back to back Bloch's *Feudal Society* and Susan Reynolds' important book *Fiefs and Vassals: The Medieval Evidence Reinterpreted*, which appeared in 1994 and is, significantly, dedicated to Brown. Reynolds offers a full and insightful analysis of the fief and of what we would once have called 'feudal' relationships in western Europe by carefully discussing their varying significance at different times and places, in the process demonstrating that it is possible to explore the topic fully without having to turn 'feudal' into 'medieval', and 'feudalism' into the leitmotif for a whole civilization.

If we can scale down the use of the word 'feudal', then perhaps we can aspire to do something similar with 'medieval'. Perhaps we can even think about getting rid of the word altogether. This would not be iconoclasm for its own sake, for the benefits for scholars, students and general readers alike would be considerable and enduring. If we abolished the terms 'medieval' and 'Middle Ages' tomorrow, the important thing would be not to find alternative labels that simply filled the same mental spaces. Instead, in our brave new 'post-medieval' world we would have to learn to live with a large repertoire of overlapping, perhaps even conflicting, labels relating to much smaller slices of time. Perhaps we could set ourselves an upper limit of 150–200 years for the duration of any one period label, simply in order to wean ourselves off the instinctive sense that history around this time comes in large chunks. We could restrict ourselves to chronological designations such as 'tenth-century France' and 'late fourteenth-century Florence' in the interests of being as neutral as possible. Or if we wanted to be more evocative, we could aim to develop systems of labels, building on those already in use as subsets of 'medieval', that jarringly cut across disciplinary boundaries. This would serve as a constant reminder that the splitting of the experiences of the societies we are studying into various categories such as political, cultural, economic, literary and intellectual, says much more about modern divisions of scholarly labour than it does about the past itself. Thus, we could apply periodizations originating in architectural or iconographic history to the study of politics, or terms derived from monastic history to the study of the agrarian economy.

The effect of all this change would no doubt be unsettling, but it would demonstrate how all facets of history join up, and it would expose the ways in which existing labelling regimes are often the unwanted traces of redundant academic turf wars. There would probably be a period of labelling anarchy before a consensus emerged within and beyond the academic community about which words to use and why. And one likely result of this in the shorter term would be a haemorrhaging of public interest away from the period formerly known as medieval, and towards other historical eras that clung on to their reassuringly familiar brand names. But the benefits in the long run would be enormous. We would be liberated from a conceptual framework that conceals more than it reveals, and we would be open to explore new, unvoiced, possibilities without worrying that we always have to justify ourselves in relation to one dominant chronological construct. In short, it would be nice to be able to say without a trace of irony that the Middle Ages never existed!

In an ideal world, then, we could do away with 'medieval' and 'Middle Ages', not in a spirit of hostility towards the period, but on the contrary as a recognition of the growing theoretical sophistication, methodological variety and thematic range that characterize modern medieval studies. As research into aspects of the Middle Ages develops on numerous fronts, our continued use of one catch-all set of terms looks more and more strained. It is starting to look like the triumph of packaging over content, something sold to the outside world but not believed in by its practitioners. Back in the real world, however, we have to live with what there is, not what we wish there would be. The remainder of this book will therefore continue to use 'medieval' and 'Middle Ages', subject to the proviso that they principally refer, not to the totality of what actually happened between about 500 and 1500, but to the narrative strategies and analytical frameworks that modern scholarship has inherited or devised. If approached in this limited sense, 'medieval' and 'Middle Ages' can still be used, if extremely cautiously. It is deceptively easy to slip back into assuming that there is a real relationship between a thing and the words used of it, that medieval-ness actually existed. One must always be ready to challenge this sort of assumption, and it has to be admitted that this constant process of mentally going back to basics can be wearying and unsettling. But, viewed more positively, it is also a large part of the challenge and fascination of studying what, simply for the sake of convenience, we must continue to call the medieval period.

3
The Evidence for Medieval History

We have seen in Chapter 2 that our understanding of a historical peri-od is affected by the chronological divisions that we project onto the past and the loaded terminology that we apply. Another, ultimately more fruitful, way of understanding a period is to come at it through the primary sources that it has left us. Intellectual fashions and tastes in chronological boundaries come and go, but the sources remain; and it is our interpretations of them that are the stuff of medieval history. The emergence of history as an academic discipline in the nineteenth century went hand in hand with new, more rigorous approaches to the study of historical sources, and the two things have remained insepa-rable. This means that as one develops an understanding of the history of the Middle Ages, it is always important to be alive to the issues that medieval sources raise, their potential and their limitations.

It might be supposed that working with and thinking about primary sources is a highly specialized activity that professional historians only do after years of training, not something to worry about when one is starting out in the subject. This view is actually false, though it has its defenders who maintain that sources are simply the means to the end of presenting an analysis of what happened in the past. When a histo-rian is resolving any problems that the sources present, this is, accord-ing to this approach, in the nature of a preliminary exercise which the reader does not need to see explicitly explained on the printed page. At most there will be footnotes to direct the reader to where the historian found the information that is being mobilized. This way of looking at the historian's task is in truth rather old-fashioned, not least because it encourages the idea that there is a 'real' and definitive past out there, and that the sources are simply neutral tools which equip us to discover what went on in our chosen bits of the past. Few historians today would trust wholeheartedly in either of these propositions.

In practical terms, it is very difficult to write about the Middle Ages, as about any distant or unfamiliar society, without making the primary sources part of the story itself. This is the result of the pull between two different perspectives that we bring to thinking about something like the medieval past. On the one hand, we know as a basic fact that, for all their differences from us, medieval people were living, breathing human beings; and from our own experience we are familiar with using what we see or hear or read to form judgements about others. People are, we trust, knowable, at least to some degree. On the other hand, with a subject such as medieval history we are presented with the task of understanding people by interpreting material which in its form and content seldom resembles the sources of information that we routinely use in our own lives. It is the tension between these two things which necessarily draws the sources to the surface of most writing on medieval history. Historians will seek to present the reader with more than just a version of what happened; they will interweave their reflections on historical events and processes with thoughts about the strengths and weaknesses of the primary material, how it came into being, why it permits certain conclusions and excludes others, and where it leaves gaps in our knowledge. The density of this interweaving will vary from one piece of historical writing to another, and often within a single book or article, depending on the nature of the argument that is being advanced. Yet it is so embedded in medieval historiographical practice that it is important to be alive to it constantly.

When medieval history developed as a university subject in the nineteenth century, its practitioners were not starting entirely from scratch. They were able to build on the work of scholars and antiquaries between the sixteenth and eighteenth centuries who had developed increasingly sophisticated techniques to understand medieval sources. Even today this work feeds through into the shape and feel of medieval history as an intellectual and technical enterprise. Probably the most important individual contribution was made by Jean Mabillon (1632–1707). As a young man, Mabillon joined the French order of monks known as the Maurists. This organization attached great importance to scholarship as part of its religious calling, and although it was only a recent foundation (the order was formed in 1618) it took a great interest in the history of the more distant past. Mabillon joined the Maurist monastery of Saint-Germain-des-Prés near Paris, where he came under the influence of one of the greatest scholars of his day, Luc d'Achery (1609–1685). Saint-Germain provided an exceptional research environment. It had a superb library which held large collections of manuscripts and books that had once belonged to rich medieval monasteries such as Corbie. And the Maurists would complement their in-house studies with field trips, or 'literary journeys', to visit other libraries and monasteries in France and some neighbouring countries.

Mabillon was one of the stars of this community of mobile scholar-monks, his researches leading to many publications. His greatest and most enduring achievement was his *De re diplomatica libri VI* [Six Books about Diplomatic], which appeared in 1681. The word 'diplomatic' as a noun is only indirectly connected to what we understand by 'diploma-cy'. It derives from the Greek for a folded document, and it has come to mean the technical study of documents, especially those such as charters, writs and wills which were created to have some legal force. In *De re diplomatica libri VI*, Mabillon set out various ways in which one could analyze a document, by looking, for example, at the handwriting (the style of which varied across time and from place to place), the technical formulae used and the style of the language, and internal evidence such as information about the date of the document. Mabillon's work continues to be the basis for research methods even today, though his techniques have been refined and expanded to accommodate new questions. For example, the great German scholar Theodor von Sickel (1826–1908) pioneered techniques which scrutinized medieval documents not just as words on a page but as cultural objects in their own right, artefacts which contain clues about the material and technological circumstances in which they were created. The study of diplomatic has moreover expanded to contribute techniques and approaches to the study of more literary rather than strictly documentary sources, for example letters and chronicles. It is perhaps the nearest thing to a defining feature of academic medieval history, though it should be emphasized that its methods are not uniquely applicable to this field: historians working on late antique and early modern history have fruitfully applied similar techniques and pose similar questions of their material.

Medievalists remain the true heirs of Mabillon and the other pioneers of source analysis because of a peculiarity of the medieval source base that has come down to us, the large number of forgeries. The word 'forgery' today conjures up lurid images of criminals committing serious fraud, but it is important to expand the scope of the word when thinking about the activities and aims of medieval forgers. There were indeed medieval equivalents of modern fraudsters using false documents to cheat their victims, but in many instances the circumstances and the degree of criminal intent were less clear-cut. It often happened, for example, that an institution such as a monastery found itself in a legal dispute which forced it to present proof of its ownership of a right or piece of property. The monastery stood to lose out if, as was sometimes the case, its rights had been preserved orally for many years but any documentary proof that may once have existed had been lost. A document purporting to be the original grant of the claimed property by a monarch or pope would then be created to fill that gap, not necessarily or mainly in a spirit of trying to cheat someone else out of his or her rights, but in order to validate the justice of one's own case. The document would not be a title deed in the modern sense of the word, but a reinforcement of an existing collective memory. It is not surprising to discover that forgeries were often stimulated by periods of disruptive change. French monasteries that had lost properties because of the Viking raids in the ninth century, for example, sometimes forged documents to re-establish their rights when they set about trying to recoup their losses. Similarly, the Norman Conquest of England wrought enormous changes in the ownership of the land, and in this state of flux the main land-owning survivors from the old order, the monasteries and major churches, sometimes fabricated documents in order to protect their rights, in some instances replacing genuine records which were no longer useful because they were written in Old English, which ceased to be a language of law and government soon after the Normans arrived.

Dealing with the problem of forgery does not simply involve sieving out genuine material from the false. Many documents are hybrids created by a scribe adapting a genuine original. And even when a document is self-evidently a forgery, it still retains a great deal of historical interest because it is evidence for what the forger was trying to achieve as well as for contemporary cultural attitudes towards the past, the status of writing, and public authority. The further back one goes in the Middle Ages, the greater the problem. Forged public documents such as the charters issued by emperors and kings and the privileges granted by popes survive in disproportionate numbers because, of course, forgers stood to gain most by producing documents in these exalted figures' names. It has been estimated that nearly half of the surviving charters issued by the Frankish Merovingian kings in the seventh and eighth centuries are forged or textually compromised. Of the 270 or so surviving charters in the name of the Frankish king and emperor Charlemagne (768–814), about 100 are false. By the time one gets to the diplomas of the German king and emperor Frederick Barbarossa (1152–90), only about 6% of the extant documents in his name are clearly forged or altered, while the status of about another 3% is uncertain.

The problem, then, slowly recedes, but it never disappears entirely, a point reinforced by the continued forging of medieval documents in the post-medieval era. Perhaps the most notorious case took place in mid-nineteenth-century France. In the late 1830s and early 1840s the French king Louis Philippe (1830–48) had part of the palace of Versailles converted into a series of galleries celebrating French history. Part of this plan involved the creation of a space glorifying French families which had distinguished themselves on the crusades, the idea being that these families would be represented by a coat of arms provided they could offer documentary proof of their crusading antecedents. The half-century since the Revolution, however, had severely disrupted the aristocratic elite in France: the old families that survived had often lost many of their records, and parvenu families were trying to claim bogus *ancien régime* pedigrees in order to enhance their status under the July Monarchy. The potential to make a killing was spotted by a chancer operating on the fringes of high society named Eugène-Henri Courtois. Courtois and his associate Paul Le Tellier, a draftsman who supplied the technical know-how, set up a forgery business producing what purported to be medieval documents that placed someone's supposed ancestor on crusade, as well as further documentation intended to establish a link between the 'crusader' and the present-day client. Courtois and Le Tellier brought to their work a strange combination of technical guile and naïve clumsiness. They had insider contacts working in the French national archives who were able to smuggle real medieval documents out to them, because they knew that for the best results they needed to cannibalize genuine medieval parchment and seals. On the other hand, some of their attempts to replicate medieval styles of handwriting were bizarrely inept. Nonetheless the deceptions often worked, and many of the forged documents found their way into official archives as well as family collections. It was only in the 1950s that the full extent of the fraud was exposed, and even then there was great indignation on the part of some of the descendants of Courtois's clients because their family traditions had come to treat the charters as the genuine article. It is probable that even today there are Courtois forgeries out there in archives and libraries waiting to catch the unwary.

The number of Courtois forgeries runs to several hundreds. In the great scheme of things, therefore, they represent only a tiny fraction of the amount of the material that is, or purports to be, about the Middle Ages. Nonetheless the Courtois case is a good, because disconcertingly late and vivid, illustration of the shifting, provisional quality of what we take to be the medieval source base at any given moment. Material that is currently accepted as genuine might in the future be exposed as a fabrication; and likewise documents currently categorized as forgeries might be reassessed. New material can come to light. New techniques can be devised to make familiar sources yield new types of information and support new interpretations. More broadly still, we should not think of medieval sources as things that were fashioned in one creative moment and then became frozen in time. Individual sources could be added to, scraped clean, copied, translated, mutilated, recycled, lost and rediscovered. Collectively, the medieval source base is a like an old building which has mutated over many centuries through a constant process of addition, demolition, and alteration. Medieval historians today have to work with the cumulative consequences of millions of often casual decisions, made over many centuries, about what to throw away and what to keep, and, if the latter, how to keep it. This means that it is important to be aware of how and why the medieval record has survived, because this ultimately determines the sorts of medieval history that we can and cannot produce.

In theory, the only limits on the sorts of sources that a medieval historian can use are set by what happens to survive. One of the most exciting and positive trends in medieval history in recent decades has been a broadening of the source repertoire and a corresponding openness to the techniques and perspectives of scholars working in other disciplines such as archaeology, architectural history, art history, music, and numismatics (the study of coins). That said, and as the importance that we still attach to the achievements of pioneers such as Mabillon and von Sickel illustrates, written materials remain the core source base for most medieval historians most of the time. Contrary to a common misconception, there is in fact a large amount of written evidence from the Middle Ages, though, as we shall see, it is unevenly distributed across space and time and is limited in the sorts of human activities that it can illuminate. When we consider how medieval written sources have come down to us, we encounter a fascinating tension in the interplay of different forces, some helping evidence to survive, and others working towards the disappearance of the traces of the past.

There are various ways in which writing can be preserved. It can, for example, be inscribed on the surface of a durable material such as metal or stone, and this can be of enormous value as evidence. In some areas of research, for example ancient Roman history, stone inscriptions are a major part of the overall source repertoire that is available to scholars. Many inscriptions in stone also survive from the Middle Ages, but by this point most of our written evidence is preserved on the page. The normal surface for making permanent written records in the classical world had been papyrus, which is made from reeds woven tightly together. It continued in use in some parts of Europe until the seventh century, and later still in a few exceptional environments such as the popes' writing office. The problem with papyrus is that it is very fragile: where it has survived in large quantities, this tends to be because it has been preserved in dry and undisturbed environments such as in the sand of the Egyptian desert. Early medieval European examples are fairly few. At the other end of the Middle Ages, paper, which had been originally developed in China, began to reach western Europe, particularly Mediterranean areas with trading contacts with the Muslim world, in the eleventh and twelfth centuries. It was only in the thirteenth and fourteenth centuries that European papermills began to be set up to produce paper on a significant scale for the domestic market, and even then it took the development of printing in the fifteenth century to secure paper's status as the standard medium for the written word. Until the recent development of durable acid-free papers, moreover, paper represents a very mixed blessing for the historian because it can easily decay and crumble if not carefully conserved.

Between the disappearance of papyrus and the gradual appearance of paper, medieval Europe's staple material for writing was parchment, which is made by scraping animal hides. This is very good news for the medieval historian, for although parchment is organic like papyrus and paper, and vulnerable to the same sorts of threats from damp, fire, insects and vermin, it is a remarkably robust material which combines flexibility and toughness. In fact these qualities have sometimes been its undoing. In the era of muskets and front-loading cannon, for example, it was discovered that parchment was very good for making gunpowder cartridges because it was pliable, light and water-resistant. In the late eighteenth century, the French revolutionary government was recycling old documents on an industrial scale at its main arsenal in Metz. As Chateaubriand, whom we encountered in Chapter 1 as a critic and victim of the Revolution, dryly remarked, the vestiges of the past glory of France were simply being blasted into oblivion out of the mouths of gun barrels. Changes in military technology and a growing sense of the importance of conservation eventually reduced this particular danger, though parchment remained vulnerable to other threats. In more recent times, for example, there was a vogue for lampshades made from recycled medieval documents! Despite all the dangers to which parchment can be exposed, however, it is no exaggeration to say that it and the stone in buildings represent the two main ways in which the civilization of the Middle Ages has materially come down to us. In other words, its physical durability is effectively the foundation on which the modern study of the medieval past is built.

A further important factor favouring the survival of medieval sources is the use of Latin as western Europe's main language of written communication. Latin's central importance to medieval civilization often strikes people as puzzling. Why, one might ask, did the Middle Ages persist so long in using a 'dead' language which should by rights have disappeared when the western half of the Roman empire came to an end? The answer depends, in fact, on what one means by dead. As we saw in Chapter 2, people in the early medieval West experienced no single moment of definitive rupture from the Roman past, and late Roman civilization fed through into medieval Europe in innumerable ways. Latin, therefore, remained a living presence, especially within the Church, which was very conscious of its roots in the Roman past and regarded Latin as a sacred language (the Bible had been translated into Latin in the late Roman period). In many parts of early medieval Europe people spoke Romance languages descended from Latin; and even in those places where the local vernacular was not Romance, Latin was kept alive by networks of educated monks and clerics. The way that Latin worked in medieval culture was not like, for example, a modern computer language that is fully understood by a small elite and utterly incomprehensible to everyone else. Although only a minority of people, mostly male, received a Latin education, within this privileged elite there were different degrees of familiarity and usage. Some had enough Latin to deal with formulaic documents and the more repetitive phrases said or sung in church services. Some were able to write in Latin, often to a very high standard. Some could even speak it; although those who could converse in the language were only a minority within a minority, this skill was significant because it helps to explain, for example, how the popes' court could deal with litigants from across western Christendom, and how international religious orders, which proliferated in the twelfth and thirteenth centuries, were able to organize annual general meetings which attracted members drawn from across Latin Christendom.

Latin aided communication across time as well as across space. This is a fundamentally important consideration when we think about how and why medieval texts have come down to us. When we picture medieval scribes at their painstaking work, the chances are, in fact, that they would have been copying an existing text rather than composing an original work. Many medieval texts survive not in their original form but as copies, or as copies of copies, and so on down sometimes long and intricate chains. The earlier the original composition, the greater the likelihood that we are now reliant on later copies; and the greater the number of copies made, of course, the greater the chances that at least one has survived the hazards of time. More than anything else, Latin made these chains possible. Imagine, say, a scribe in an English monastery in 1100 copying out a chronicle that was originally written in 800 in what later became France. If the original had been in the vernacular spoken by its author, it would have been incomprehensible to the later copyist and his potential readership, and there would have been no practical reason to bother with it in the first place. But by virtue of its being in Latin, the chronicle could sustain a sense of interest and relevance across otherwise impermeable geographical, cultural and chronological boundaries. If the 1100 copy is the only one to survive, modern historians working on the period around 800 will clearly be in the copyist's debt for preserving an important source. And even if the original version survives, and the 1100 text is a slavish copy that adds no extra information drawn from other sources, the later version will still retain immense value as an object in its own right, because it can tell us something about the cultural environment in which it was produced. What does the fact that an English monk would take the time to copy out a 300-year-old chronicle reveal about attitudes towards historical writing in particular and the past in general in his own day?

The sense of continuity to which our imagined scribe in 1100 would have been bearing witness was reinforced by the status accorded to works written in the heyday of Roman literature. As is well known, most surviving pieces of Roman literature survive thanks to the work of medieval copyists. When these copies were being made, it was not in a spirit of preserving the vestiges of the past for their own sake, or at least not mainly so. The texts continued to speak to their medieval readerships in various ways, despite being for the most part the work of people who were writing before the emergence and spread of Christianity. In addition, these texts served as models of good style that could be successfully extended into cultural environments that were very unlike those in which they had originally been written. The works of the Roman historians Sallust and Suetonius, for example, exerted an enormous influence on medieval writers of history. The continued existence of Roman works as exemplars of good practice meant, moreover, that periodically efforts could be made to halt any drift in Latin usage away from its classical roots, and to restore what was seen as the proper purity of the language. This rebooting of classical Latin was a central element in the 'renaissances' of the ninth and twelfth centuries which anticipated many of the literary and linguistic interests of Renaissance humanists in the fifteenth and sixteenth centuries. By the twelfth century (and earlier in a few exceptional cases such as Anglo-Saxon England), one begins to encounter a growing body of material written in versions of the vernacular languages spoken by ordinary people. Much of this output is literary in nature, including historical writings as well as poetry and songs, but one increasingly comes across documentary material in the vernacular as well. Nonetheless, even as the vernaculars were growing in status and finding more new applications, Latin remained the single most important language of written communication up to the end of the Middle Ages, and indeed beyond in many learned, legal and administrative contexts. Medieval Latin was anything but dead.

Without the staying power of parchment as a material and of Latin as a medium of communication, our evidence for the Middle Ages would be immeasurably thinner. Even so, it is important to recognize that the difference between what we have now and what once existed is truly staggering. In his ground-breaking work *From Memory to Written Record: England 1066–1307*, Michael Clanchy estimates that only 1% of the documents that were produced in England in the two and a half centuries covered by his study still survive. This figure is all the more sobering when one bears in mind that England had relatively well-developed administrative and legal systems that, person for person, generated more records than most other parts of medieval Europe, and by extension encouraged people to make an effort to preserve records carefully. In addition, England since the Middle Ages has been relatively untouched by the revolutions and wars that have had such a harmful effect on the survival rate of historical records in many other parts of Europe.

The rate of attrition has been formidable and, until the development in the nineteenth century of the institutionalized archiving and conserving of material, unrelenting. Some of our most important sources hang by the slenderest of manuscript threads. *The Ecclesiastical History* by the twelfth-century Anglo-Norman monk Orderic Vitalis, for example, is a major source for English and northern French history, but its manuscript survival has been precarious. Not many copies seem to have been made during and soon after Orderic's lifetime. It would have taken just a small fire, a flash flood, some hungry rodents, or the passing attentions of a looting soldier, and the manuscript chain would have been severely compromised, if not broken forever. Some texts have fared particularly badly, with the result that we have to rely on copies made by early modern scholars and antiquaries. It is only by this means, for example, that we still have the chronicle of another twelfth-century historian, Geoffrey of Vigeois, whose work is particularly valuable because he was writing in southern France, an area which on the whole did not produce much in the way of historical writing. The only known medieval manuscripts of two texts that are central to our understanding of Anglo-Saxon England, Aethelweard's chronicle and the biography of Alfred the Great by Asser, were lost, substantially and wholly respectively, in the calamitous fire at Ashburnham House in 1731 which tore through the collection of medieval material assembled by the antiquarian Sir Robert Cotton (1571–1631).

The story of the survival of medieval records is a mixture of positives and negatives. On the plus side, there are some basic physical realities working in our favour. Texts can be copied and the copies dispersed, thereby increasing the chances of survival. Written material is also compact: a few shelves, a chest or a cupboard, could store documents which, when presented in modern printed editions, will run to many dozens of volumes. This could cut both ways: one fire or flood would suffice to wipe out great numbers of sources at a stroke, but packing written material together also increased the chances of its surviving in a relatively dry, undisturbed environment. Just as importantly, the written word has long enjoyed a privileged status in Western culture. Learning to read and write has usually been the cornerstone of educational programmes, whereas other forms of literacy, such as the ability to read music or to interpret the iconography of paintings, have tended to be seen as valuable but not necessary accomplishments. People have long been used to the idea of referring to writing to decide important matters such as a case being tried before a court. In these circumstances, medieval records were often preserved in the centuries immediately following the Middle Ages thanks to an almost instinctive respect for writing in itself. It is noteworthy that in the eighteenth and nineteenth centuries official efforts to conserve medieval Europe's written records generally began earlier, and met with greater success, than the equivalent movements to preserve the Middle Ages' artistic and architectural remains.

On the negative side, however, early modern antiquaries and institutions tended to be selective in what medieval records they preserved.

Their interests were usually teleological: that is to say, they were mostly concerned with medieval texts to the extent that they helped to explain some aspect of their contemporary experience, such as the operations of English common law and the English constitution, the liturgy and customs of the Catholic Church, the origins of saints' cults, an aristocratic family's lands and titles, or the commercial and legal privileges of a civic corporation. It was only with the establishment of state-run archives in the nineteenth century that the idea took firm hold that the records of the distant past should be preserved just because they might be useful to a researcher at an unspecified date in the future, irrespective of the significance attached to them at that particular moment.

This principle of 'just in case' is fundamentally important, because a great deal of medieval evidence, especially after around 1200, is routine bureaucratic material with numerous repetitive formulae and long lists. These are not glamour sources like chronicles, and it takes more of an act of faith to spend time and money preserving them for the benefit of unborn generations of researchers applying as-yet-uninvented methodologies. Before this principle took root, however, a great deal of material was discarded for being irrelevant and impenetrable. And even when a document made it into a state-run archive, there were further dangers to face: misshelving, poor environmental control, the wear and tear of regular handling, even theft. Sometimes the best of intentions backfired; it is not uncommon today to be confronted with a piece of medieval parchment that looks like it has been covered with black paint. This is the unforeseen long-term result of the once common archivist's trick of applying chemical agents to the surface of parchment in order to make faded ink stand out more clearly.

These are the perils, however, of that small proportion of the medieval evidence that has managed to survive in the first place. Most sources have not been so lucky, and the centuries since the Middle Ages are a catalogue of man-made and natural disasters that have eaten away at the evidence. Perhaps the most infamous case of the destruction of medieval sources is one of the most recent; it took place in Italy during the Second World War, a time and a place, that is to say, in which the principle of just-in-case archival preservation was firmly established. The Archivio di Stato, or state archive, in Naples held one of the most important and extensive collections of later medieval material anywhere in Europe. Southern Italy in the Middle Ages had had a rich and varied history. In the eleventh and twelfth centuries it had been ruled by Normans who had built on the local Latin and Greek traditions, as well as the Muslim culture they encountered in Sicily, to develop a remarkably sophisticated government structure. It is sometimes said that the complexity of their political, administrative and legal apparatus was only surpassed by their cousins in Norman England (though other areas such as Catalonia in north-eastern Spain equally stand out). The Norman legacy was in turn built on by the Hohenstaufen dynasty of German kings who acquired Norman Italy at the end of the twelfth century, and then by the Angevins, a branch of the French royal family that defeated and replaced the Hohenstaufen in the 1260s. The cumulative result was a very substantial collection of material from the thirteenth century onwards, as well as some very valuable earlier documents.

During the War it became clear that the Archivio was vulnerable to bombing, and so early in 1943 the greater part of its oldest material was moved to a seventeenth-century country house, the Villa Montesano, near Nola. In addition to many files and volumes, 866 cases of material containing tens of thousands of manuscripts and dossiers were packed and transported. The decision to make the move was vindicated by the fact that the Archivio buildings back in Naples were badly damaged in several air raids over the course of the next few months. By September 1943, however, the War was starting to catch up with the remote villa and its precious contents. The Allies had invaded southern Italy and were gradually fighting their way up the peninsula. The Germans opposing them were faced with the loss of their former Italian allies. Meanwhile, Italian partisans were becoming more daring and effective in their guerrilla tactics. The German forces around Nola began to feel the pressure, executing Italian officers whose loyalty they no longer commanded and taking retaliatory action against local people if the partisans made an attack on them. When a German soldier was killed near San Paolo Belsito, the village close to the Villa Montesano, the leading figures in the village were rounded up to be shot. They were only saved at the last minute, thanks to the desperate pleas of a German woman who was married to a local man. In return for their lives, the villagers promised to hand over the person responsible for the soldier's murder in the next 24 hours; but they only darkened the Germans' mood still further by melting into the countryside overnight. In the meantime small parties of German soldiers were beginning to sniff around the villa and ask awkward questions about the contents of the cases. It is possible that they suspected that partisans were using the cases to hide their weapons. By 29 September the director in charge of the archive had become so worried that he tried to send a letter to the local German commander in Nola pleading for the protection of his material, and pointing out that some of the sources, in particular a precious volume containing copies of documents issued by the German emperor Frederick II between 1239 and 1240, were in effect records of German history.

The letter was overtaken by events, however. On the morning of the 30th a junior German officer and two other soldiers rode up to the villa on motorcycles and told the horrified curators that they had orders to destroy the cases. Turning a deaf ear to all the desperate entreaties, they then set fire to all the material. Brave attempts were made to retrieve at least a few items, but the smoke soon drove the rescuers back. Only a tiny fraction of the material was saved. It remains a mystery who the soldiers were and who, if anyone, had given them the order. It is easy to condemn the perpetrators of this piece of wanton destruction, but one should bear in mind the heady mix of fear, vindictiveness and indifference that can overtake combatants in stressful situations. This was, after all, a war zone; the Allies advanced into the area just two days later. There were many examples of cultural vandalism on all sides from the War, some of it a matter of private initiative, some the collateral effects of strategic and tactical necessity. A few months after this incident, for example, and during the same southern Italian campaign, the Allies were faced with the task of taking Montecassino, a site of the foremost cultural significance because of its association with St Benedict of Nursia, the father of Western monasticism. Montecassino occupies high ground, control of which was vital to both sides. In the end the Allies bombed the monastery complex into rubble, and even then had no choice but to compound the destruction by weeks of bitter fighting on the ground.

The history of medieval sources is also full of alarming near-misses. One of the closest shaves happened to the Bayeux Tapestry during the ferment of the French Revolution. The Tapestry is one of the most famous and recognizable of medieval artefacts. It is not a tapestry, in fact, but a woollen embroidery on several linen panels sewn end to end. In its surviving state it is about 70 metres long; the original was longer, possibly substantially so. As is well known, it tells the story of the Norman conquest of England. It begins with the journey of the future King Harold to France, where he enters into an agreement with Duke William of Normandy concerning the succession to the ailing King Edward the Confessor. It then depicts Harold's repudiation of the agreement when Edward dies, his assumption of the English throne, William's preparations for the invasion of England, and the invasion itself culminating in the defeat and death of Harold at Hastings. The

Tapestry has achieved iconic status: it dominates visualizations of the Norman Conquest in particular and the Norman period in general. It is also so detailed in its narrative that it has come to enjoy the status of an honorary written source, which is fitting because its designer probably drew on written accounts of the Conquest, and the Tapestry in turn became a source for later writers.

The fact that the Tapestry has come down to us, however, is itself extraordinary. In 1792 an invasion scare gripped France and there were musters of troops around the country, including in the Norman town of Bayeux, where the Tapestry was stored in the cathedral. It was discovered that there were too few awnings to cover the militia's wagons, so it was decided to take the Tapestry and cut it into pieces in order to provide coverings. This practical solution had the added attraction of being a politically symbolic statement. A mood of iconoclasm was in the air: earlier that year the French revolutionary government had enacted that works of art and documents that evoked the spirit of the old monarchist regime should be destroyed. The story told by the Tapestry was not about the French monarchy as such, but it is easy to see how its evocative images of aristocratic and royal power could nonetheless offend revolutionary sensibilities. The Tapestry was removed from the cathedral and placed on a wagon. It was only saved by the prompt action of a prominent citizen, Lambert Léonard-Leforestier, who served in the local government and was a former *commissaire de police*. He had the order to destroy the Tapestry reversed, and stood up to the crowd, soothing its iconoclastic ardour. This was not the end of the Tapestry's perils, however. A short time later it survived a proposal to have it cut up for display in a revolutionary civic festival. As late as the Second World War it came close to destruction more than once. During the liberation of Paris in August 1944, even as fierce fighting was raging in the streets, an attempt was made by the SS, probably on behalf of its cultural division the *Ahnenerbe* (the historical basis, incidentally, for the villains in two of the *Indiana Jones* movies), to spirit the Tapestry out of the Louvre, where it was being stored in a cellar, and back to Germany. If this attempt had succeeded, it is almost certain that the Tapestry would have been lost in the chaos of the last months of the War.

The misadventures of the Naples archive and the Bayeux Tapestry are particularly vivid illustrations of a process of attrition that has been going on since the Middle Ages themselves. It is also important to remember that the written sources that have survived are by no means a random and fully representative sample of what once existed. We have proportionately more of the deluxe end of the manuscript range, items produced to last, than we do of hastily written scribbles which served an immediate purpose but had no long-term value. A great deal of medieval writing was in fact done not with pen and ink on parchment but with a stylus on wax tablets, which served as notebooks. Unsurprisingly, very few examples have survived. More even than this, our very reliance on written records from the medieval past has a distorting effect, because, even though writing could on occasion touch the lives of people surprisingly low down the social and educational pecking order, we are for the most part dealing with societies which functioned orally. It is important not to equate oral culture with a lack of sophistication. Even those elements of medieval civilization in which literacy and writing mattered a great deal, such as monasteries, were also the sites of lively and complex oral cultures. Often, when a particular type of medieval source begins to become plentiful, this is not a sign that something significantly new is happening, but simply that someone has begun to commit to writing the sort of information, such as the decisions of a local court or the dues owed by a tenant farmer to his landlord, that up till then people had carried around in their heads and passed on orally. The fact that the information was now being put into writing is itself important, but the corresponding shifts in people's underlying lived experience might have been quite minor, with the written evidence simply supplementing ways of remembering and communicating information that continued to be predominantly oral in nature.

The written sources for the Middle Ages also contain several in-built imbalances. They are much more likely to have been written by a man, and to say more about men than women. They say more about adults than children. They are much more likely to feature high-status people: the wealthiest, the most powerful, or the best educated. The sources tell us more about the life of the Church than about secular affairs (though the distinction between the two was much hazier than in a modern Western society). They tell us far more about life played out in the public domain than in the private. And although medieval thinkers had a sense of history playing itself out over the long term, in practical terms most medieval sources bear upon particular events or short periods rather than long-term processes such as demographic change or economic growth. Another noteworthy feature of the source base is that it leans heavily towards representing life as it ought to be rather than how it was in practice. This is most obviously true of the normative, or standard-setting, material that has survived such as the Rules that governed life in monasteries or law codes issued in the name of kings: this sort of material has a significant place in our source repertoire, especially for the earlier parts of the Middle Ages. But the same can also apply to material that on the surface appears to describe specific and unique slices of lived reality. When, for example, a chronicle describes the actions of a king on one particular day, it is highly unlikely that what we are seeing is a piece of neutral, fly-on-the-wall observation, even supposing that the chronicler was close in space and time to the events he is describing. The chronicler's version of what happened and his reflections on his subject's motivations will be filtered through contemporary expectations about the roles that kings were expected to play and an awareness of the ideological underpinnings of royal status. The description will thus be about generic 'king-ness' in motion as least as much as it individuates one human being doing something specific and unrepeatable on one particular day in history. The same sort of consideration applies to the ways in which sources tend to present women, or the clergy, or the poor, or different occupations and classes, or Jews and Muslims. It also applies to material which on the face of it looks the most overtly descriptive in nature, such as a list of rents owed to a landowner, a list of the knights whose services were available to a ruler, or a brief memorandum of a judgement reached in a trial: even in these sorts of ostensibly bald sources one is in fact encountering a constant tension between the ideal and the real. As much as anything, this is a reminder that medieval people were not, of course, creating records for the benefit of historians in the distant future, but in response to their own needs, which included bringing a sense of order and shape to their world.

It should be emphasized that the imbalances within the source base are in the nature of tendencies rather than absolutes. There are many exceptions such as a substantial body of material written by women, and sources such as inquisitorial records and the accounts of miracles believed to have been experienced by pilgrims at saints' shrines, which lift the lid a little on the world of the poor and powerless majority of the population. To a limited extent the imbalances also begin to flatten out when the amount and range of the surviving source material expand significantly around 1200. The year 1200 should not be taken as a hard and fast date: in some areas such as England and Catalonia the documentary boom begins earlier, in others later. But generally speaking it is around this time that the quantity and diversity of the sources at our disposal are transformed. There are several reasons for this. One is a growth of political power at the royal or equivalent centre in most parts of western Europe, which brought with it an increase in bureaucracy and a corresponding demand for bureaucrats educated in the newly emerging schools and universities. Crucially, governments started to learn the value of keeping comprehensive records of their financial, administrative and judicial business, and just as importantly of finding places to keep them so that they were no longer vulnerable to the sort of mishap that happened in 1194 when many of the records of French royal government, which travelled around with the king, were lost in one day when the king was defeated in battle at Fréteval.

Another factor to consider is the growth in the power and resources of the Church, which from the middle of the eleventh century had begun to reform its organization in order to enhance its influence over all levels of society. The growth in the number and size of towns from the eleventh and twelfth centuries is yet another significant factor, for the commercial and legal culture fostered in urban environments encouraged the creation and preservation of more and fuller written records. The transformation in the source base around 1200 is so significant that it should in fact be added to the list of arguments in Chapter 2 undermining the unrealistic homogeneity implied by the terms 'Middle Ages' and 'medieval'. A scholar working on European history around, say, 700 is doing something wholly different from another scholar working on 1400: the sources at their disposal do not simply introduce differences of scale, but also fundamental qualitative judgements about who and what can be studied and the sort of questions that can realistically be answered. In this respect, the late medievalist will often have much more in common with someone working on 1600, 1700 or even 1800.

If all medieval people most of the time, and most medieval people all of the time, were able to go about their lives without their actions registering in the written record, and if we also bear in mind the enormous amount of material that has been lost, it follows that we have to be very cautious when written evidence is, exceptionally, available. A good case in point is the history of aristocratic families in the central medieval period, say, between the ninth and thirteenth centuries. It was largely from the ranks of these families that the Church recruited the monks, nuns and clerics who were educated to join the literate elite: the very elite, that is to say, which was responsible for the great majority of the written sources that have come down to us. To this extent, then, we know a good deal about the aristocracy because of its links to the Church. But most members of the aristocracy who did not join the

Church did not receive the same sort of education. Some, women as well as men, may have had a passive knowledge of rudimentary Latin, and some would have been able to read vernacular texts. On the whole, however, these would have been peripheral skills, nice to have but not fundamental to day-to-day living. Apart from the very stylized pictures of themselves that aristocrats heard or read in verse epics and courtly romances, theirs was not a culture that routinely went about its business and fashioned its own self-image through the medium of writing. In the relative absence of sources *by* aristocrats about themselves (there is much more of this sort of material from later in the Middle Ages, in fact), research into these people has to look elsewhere.

In recent decades the staple resources exploited by historians working in this field have been charters which record property transactions between an aristocratic family and a religious institution such as a monastery or large church (which in almost all cases is the party whose attempts to preserve the document mean that it now survives). The standard pattern was for an aristocrat to give (or sometimes sell, lease or mortgage) rights or property to the church in return for prayers for his or her soul and the souls of family members. These documents survive in large numbers (although their geographical distribution is patchy) and from them historians have been able to extract a great deal of information about aristocratic family structure, the social significance that attached to the various words used to express someone's status, the different ways in which landed estates were exploited, and a host of other issues. Without these sources, large chunks of our knowledge would simply disappear. On the other hand, these documents are not casual snapshots of a family caught going about its mundane routines. They are highly stylized and formulaic witnesses to a few unrepresentative and unusually highly charged occasions. Many donations to churches were made at solemn, liminal moments, such as when a lord was dying or was departing on a crusade, or when an heir was entering into his inheritance and wished to demonstrate his new status through participation in public rituals. Many 'gifts' were in fact resolutions of property disputes. The family members who gathered to witness a gift to a church were not necessarily one domestic unit: their membership of the family group for the purposes of the document amounted to a public act, not a statement of routine identity. Aristocratic culture in this period, like all medieval cultures, was largely oral. When written evidence, unusually, cuts into this orality, we have to be particularly careful not to exaggerate or distort the lessons that can be learned from it.

At least in the case of aristocratic families there is a realistic expectation of finding substantial, if perhaps problematic, bodies of evidence. The same cannot be said of the great mass of the medieval population. Viewed as unique, flesh-and-blood individuals, most of the people who lived in western Europe between about 500 and 1500 are now historically non-existent. They are literally nameless; they have slipped through the documentary net either because they were never caught by it in the first place or because the documents that once mentioned them have long since disappeared. There are no extensive parish records of births, marriages and deaths to speak of before the sixteenth century. There are no gravestones for the poor until later still. Their physical remains are mostly atomized beyond archaeological reach. These medieval people are completely and utterly gone. The best that we can usually say about this anonymous multitude is that they must have existed in an abstract sense. If, for example, we know that a village was continuously inhabited over a given period, we can deduce that people of a certain sort would have been living there on a certain day even though we will never be able to discover what they were called or what they thought about their own lives and about each other. At most, these once completely real and unique people are present to us as representatives of a generic living-in-a-medieval-village-ness that we can piece together from diverse sources, most of them about different villages and from different times. The documentary darkness that has enveloped whole communities is truly sobering.

It is frankly difficult to get a clear sense of something which for the most part does not exist in the first place. So a useful way to gain a fuller understanding of the limitations of the medieval evidence is to look forward to just beyond the Middle Ages, into the sixteenth century, and to ask what, if anything, is beginning to change by that time. Needless to say, sixteenth-century history is a vast field, but we are fortunate in having two celebrated books, Natalie Zemon Davis's *The Return of Martin Guerre* (1983) and Carlo Ginzburg's *The Cheese and the Worms* (1976, English translation 1980), that together provide an excellent point of entry into questions about sources, how they came into being, what they are about, and what sorts of history can be made from them. Both books are examples of what has become known as 'microhistory', which involves looking in depth at a narrowly-defined historical subject such as the life of an individual, a small community such as a village, or even a single incident. The aim typically is to examine the actions and ideas of people whose individual experiences tend to get lost in the necessarily broad and sweeping statements that historians usually make: people, that is, who would otherwise just be faces in the crowd. Microhistory also favours looking beyond an individual's or group's material circumstances to ask questions about their perceptions of the world. This approach has been popular in recent decades as many historians have lost faith in the idea that there are big patterns to be found in human affairs across large stretches of time and place. Better, it seems, to look in as much detail as the evidence allows at everyday life on the ground, and to explore all the rich diversity that one finds there. A further attraction of microhistory is that it enables historians (if the evidence permits, and this is a big 'if') to pay close attention to the sorts of people who were marginalized in traditional politics-centred history, such as women, the poor, the uneducated, and those who dissented in some way against the norms of their society.

The Return of Martin Guerre, by the distinguished American historian Natalie Zemon Davis, concerns a story which has become quite well known because it was the subject of a 1981 French film, *Le retour de Martin Guerre,* starring a young Gérard Depardieu. Interestingly, Davis worked closely with the makers of the film as historical consultant, and her influence is evident in the very good period feel of the movie, which is set in sixteenth-century France, Davis's area of expertise. (A Hollywood adaptation, *Sommersby,* starring Richard Gere and Jodie Foster, came out in 1993; this completely shifted the story's setting, to the American South just after the Civil War, but more or less kept to the plot of the original.) Martin Guerre was a fairly prosperous peasant living in the village of Artigat in the far south of France. In 1548, after a family dispute, he left home, abandoning his wife, Bertrande de Rols, and their young son. Eight years later another man claiming to be Martin appeared on the scene. He was accepted back by the Guerre family and the village community. Crucially, Bertrande acknowledged the man as her husband; she almost certainly saw through the deception and played along with it, perhaps because the new 'Martin' was a much more congenial partner than the original. In time, however, doubts began to surface in public about the man's true identity, and in 1560 the case came to court. Just when it looked as though the impostor, who had memorized many trivial details about Martin's past life and had a very convincing manner, would succeed in swaying the judges in his favour, the real Martin Guerre dramatically reappeared as if from nowhere. The impostor, in reality a man named Arnaud du Tilh, was convicted of adultery and the fraudulent appropriation of property, and he was sentenced to death.

Davis's telling of this remarkable story is partly based on documentary evidence from Artigat and other places nearby: documents, that is to say, such as wills, leases, and contracts about the use of livestock. These are the bread-and-butter sources for the social and economic history of peasant life around this time. The documents include references to some of those who became caught up in the Martin Guerre story, such as members of the Guerre and Rols families. But the story as we know it could not be told on the basis of these sources alone. Rather, Davis uses the documentary evidence to build up a background picture of what life in mid-sixteenth-century Artigat was like for people like the Guerres and the Rols. There are also some formal records surviving from Arnaud's trial, but again these do not provide the amount of detailed information that could form the basis of a book-length reconstruction of the case (let alone a two-hour movie). For the narrative detail which occupies the foreground of Davis's reconstruction of events, she is able to draw on more exceptional pieces of evidence in the form of two books about the case that appeared soon after Arnaud's trial. One, *The Admirable History of the Pseudo-Martin of Toulouse*, was by a young lawyer named Guillaume Le Sueur. The other, and more important, work was *A Memorable Case* by Jean de Coras, a celebrated academic lawyer who was one of the judges at Arnaud's trial. Intrigued by the case and by Arnaud himself, Coras wrote up the story based on court records and what he had recently heard from witnesses during the trial. As he related the story he included numerous annotations discussing legal and moral issues that were raised by such an unusual case: for Coras this learned commentary was what the book was principally about, not simply the recording of the bare story for posterity. But thanks to his efforts, as well as those of Le Sueur, we have a wealth of information which Davis uses to excellent effect. Not that everything becomes clear: Davis wrestles, for example, with the question of what Bertrande's motives were in accepting the false Martin, an issue that was fudged at the trial in order to save her from accusations of adultery, which was treated as a very serious offence. There are also many gaps and grey areas. For example, Davis argues that one reason why Arnaud and Bertrande were happy to live together as husband and wife was that they were both Protestant sympathizers, potentially a vital lead for understanding the whole case, but a claim that some critics thought was based on flimsy evidence. Nonetheless, all this is relative. Compared to what we would normally expect to know about life in a late medieval or early modern village, and about the actions and thoughts of particular individuals living there, the case of Martin Guerre offers much more.

The Italian historian Carlo Ginzburg was one of the pioneers of microhistory (a term in fact taken from the Italian *microstoria*), and his

The Cheese and the Worms is acknowledged as a classic of the genre. Its focus is on a miller from north-eastern Italy named Domenico Scandello, or Menocchio as he was commonly known. In 1583–4 and again in 1598–9 Menocchio was investigated by the Holy Office, better known as the Inquisition, the arm of the Catholic Church charged with the rooting out of heresy. Witnesses were called, and Menocchio himself was interrogated at great length. As was a normal part of inquisitorial procedure, the witnesses' statements and the exchanges between Menocchio and his interrogators were recorded and written up, and these records survive. They are the basis of Ginzburg's remarkable investigation of Menocchio's mental world. The curious title of the book is inspired by Menocchio's attempts to find an analogy that would help to explain to his interrogators his ideas about the origins of the universe: the world and the first living things, angels, had emerged, he claimed, from a primordial chaos in the same sort of way that worms (i.e. maggots) seem to be created inside cheese. As this suggests, Menocchio had odd ideas, but there was much more to his worldview than some sort of folksy peasant wisdom. Unusually for someone with his background, Menocchio was literate and had read a number of books that had influenced his views; some of the titles came up in his interrogations. This opened up a second source base for Ginzburg, who was able to go back to the books that Menocchio mentioned and cross-match what they actually say against the ideas that Menocchio thought he had taken from them. This comparison revealed that what Menocchio brought to his reading and to his thinking about it afterwards was an odd mix of quite thoughtful interpretation, extreme selectivity, a talent for getting the wrong end of the stick, and a tendency to latch onto relatively unimportant parts of an argument, turning them into *the* main point. For Ginzburg, this was what happened when some of the bookish erudition of the educated elite was sieved through a filter in Menocchio's brain constructed from what he had learned from popular oral culture and non-elite ideas about the world.

Although these two books concern people who lived two or three generations after the conventional boundary between the medieval and early modern periods, they are invaluable reading for anyone interested in the Middle Ages. The point here is not that they illustrate an abrupt and profound break with the past. Far from it. The post-medieval historical landscape does not suddenly explode with numerous Menocchios and Arnaud du Tilhs, who were clearly unusual figures in many ways. We know so much about them because, exceptionally, representatives of society's learned, powerful elites made it their business to find out about the world of the lower classes and write up what they discovered. The simple fact that both Arnaud and Menocchio ended up being executed by the authorities itself demonstrates that they were not run-of-the-mill representatives of the faceless masses. What the cases of Menocchio the miller and the false Martin Guerre do is to provide an observation point from which we can look back into the Middle Ages and ask what it is possible to find out about the non-elite majority of the medieval population. From this vantage point, it appears that from the sixteenth century onwards the source material offers many more opportunities than do medieval sources for building historical analyses around detailed investigations of specific non-elite *individuals* – investigations, that is, not just into the sorts of external circumstances that can be retrieved from documents like wills and legal records, but also into these people's interior mental worlds. What, in other words, made these people unique, distinctive individuals rather than just representatives of an occupational group or social class? On the other hand, this opening up of new perspectives is the culmination of a process that can already be detected in the Middle Ages, especially from about 1200 as the volume and variety of the surviving sources begin to increase substantially. This means that there are at least opportunities to do for later medieval *groups* what Davis and Ginzburg were able to do with early modern individuals.

Perhaps the best-known illustration of this concerns a small and remote village in southern France called Montaillou (oddly enough, not very far from the Artigat of Martin Guerre fame). Montaillou has been catapulted into the historical limelight because its story was bound up with that of Catharism. The Cathars were followers of a form of Christianity that effectively amounted to a completely different religion from that espoused by the Catholic Church. Their message found a sympathetic audience in many parts of southern France in the later twelfth and thirteenth centuries, but they were branded as heretics and combated by the Catholic authorities, ineffectively at first but then with increasing rigour, so that by 1300 Catharism had been pushed back into remote pockets in the Pyrenean mountains, including the area around Montaillou. The villagers were investigated by the Inquisition, that is to say an earlier version of the organization that examined Menocchio's case nearly three centuries later, and the surviving records of this process are the historian's route into this village world. Inquisitorial proceedings took place between 1318 and 1325. They were led by Jacques Fournier, the bishop of Pamiers, who was a high-flyer in the Catholic Church (he subsequently became pope, as

Benedict XII, in 1334). In fact, the Church had already broken the back of heresy in the region, and all that was left was the tidying up of loose ends. Fournier and his team were nonetheless very meticulous and methodical. People accused of heresy were interrogated, as were witnesses, and their replies were recorded. One of the volumes, or registers, containing the written-up accounts of what was said survives. Tantalizingly, we know that there were once other volumes which have since been lost.

About 100 cases feature in the surviving register. Nearly all involve low-status people such as peasants and artisans. A significant number of those interrogated were women. More than a quarter of those interrogated lived in or near Montaillou itself. The interrogators posed detailed questions, and in recording the answers that they heard they preserved a wealth of detail about people's ordinary lives that would otherwise not have made it into the written record. As Fournier and his team realized, the heretical belief system that they were trying to destroy was bound up in numerous and complex ways with the whole social, economic and cultural environment of the area. Teasing out information about heresy, therefore, involved prompting those being questioned to reflect on the intricacies of their day-to-day existence, the relationships they formed, the conversations they had, the things they heard. In the process, a great deal of seemingly mundane information was recorded in order to supply the necessary context. On the basis of this information, in 1975 the French historian Emmanuel Le Roy Ladurie published an account of life in and around Montaillou (the English translation appeared in 1978). The book became a publishing sensation. Its popularity stemmed from the fact that it seemed to be able to get its readers close to the sort of people who seldom have a voice in the surviving historical record. (In France, where many people are second- or third-generation migrants from the countryside to the towns, the book also tapped into widespread feelings of nostalgia about village life and its role in French cultural identity in more recent times.) 'Voice' is an apposite term, for the way in which the depositions were recorded was in the first person, and within them recollected dialogue was typically rendered as direct speech. It almost feels as if the peasants are speaking straight to us.

But appearances can be very deceptive. Le Roy Ladurie was perhaps too trusting of people's memories of events and conversations that had sometimes taken place ten or twenty years earlier. Subsequently historians have been more alive to the very constructed nature of what the people were saying under interrogation and of the ways in which their words could be edited and tidied up when the final written record, based on notes taken during the interrogations, was compiled. Le Roy Ladurie's claim that the register reveals 'the factual history of ordinary people' is surely too sweeping, and is not in fact borne out by the book itself.[13] That said, however, the book contains a great deal of fascinating material relating to many aspects of life in Montaillou, such as the inhabitants' domestic and working environments, their family circumstances, local power structures, people's beliefs about fate and magic, body language, women's experiences, men's and women's sex lives, and people's attitudes to death and illness. Readers are often drawn to some of the more colourful individuals in the village such as the roguish priest Peter Clergue; the fact that so vivid a description was possible in his case and other cases demonstrates the extent to which we are normally starved of anything like this amount of detail, especially in relation to low-status people and the sort of small-world communities within which, after all, the great majority of medieval people lived, worked and died.

Although we have seen that the general trend is for there to be more evidence, and more types of evidence, the later in time one goes, it is important to note that this is not a hard and fast rule. An interesting feature of many aspects of medieval history, especially before the significant increase in the surviving source base around 1200, is that we sometimes have to work with clusters of material, oases in the desert that stand out conspicuously compared to what is available for other times and places. Sometimes these clusters represent a very short timeframe, perhaps only a few years. Often they relate to events in one particular place or to the ideas of one small group of people. The trick then becomes to work out how to make the most of the unusual opportunity presented by the rare clump of material. How far can the lessons drawn from it be pushed both backwards and forwards in time? How much can we extend the geographical application of the conclusions we reach from the sources? And if an individual or small community created the material, how far can we use it to form ideas about other people living in different circumstances? To a greater or lesser extent, these sorts of challenges run through all medieval history. Even quite generalized and sweeping statements about medieval civilization can prove on close inspection to be based on one or more of these source clusters, which have been pressed into service to substantiate big points extending well beyond the immediate context of when, where and why the sources came into being. As often as not, these generalizations are sound, but it is always a good idea to ask yourself whether a medieval historian making this sort of pronouncement is, in the perfectly valid interests of making the most of whatever evidence survives, stretching a source cluster too far.

An excellent illustration of an oasis in the documentary desert and of the particular challenges that it can pose comes from southern Spain around the middle of the ninth century. Between 851 and 859 nearly fifty Christians living in or near the city of Córdoba were executed by the Muslim government for blaspheming against Islam or, in a minority of cases, for apostasy, that is to say for living as Christians despite being technically Muslims according to Islamic law. The experiences of these 'martyrs', as their supporters liked to think of them, are a remarkable story and one we can trace in unusual detail thanks to the writings of two contemporary observers. Before we look at these writers in detail, however, we need to sketch a little of the background.

In 711 forces made up of Muslim Arabs and north African Berbers crossed the Straits of Gibraltar and invaded Spain. Spain was at that time a Christian kingdom under the rule of the descendants of Germanic tribesmen, the Visigoths, who had themselves taken over from the Romans in the fifth and sixth centuries. The Arab invaders swiftly broke the back of the Visigothic regime, and over the course of the eighth century they consolidated their hold on most of the peninsula, leaving a few small and, at this stage, insignificant pockets of Christian rule in the far north. The invaders became the new political and military elite, but there was little popular migration from north Africa into Spain, especially beyond the south and east of the peninsula where the Muslims had their main urban centres and their most intensively exploited agricultural land. Most of the Christians stayed put. Their situation as the numerically superior but politically inferior part of the population was thus not unlike the circumstances in which the Anglo-Saxons were to find themselves after the Norman Conquest of England in 1066. There was one big difference, however, in that for all that separated the English and the Normans in post-Conquest England, they at least shared the same Christian religion. This fundamental point of cultural contact was absent in Spain. Nonetheless, the Christians were able to accommodate themselves to the new order in various ways. Islamic law extended a degree of toleration to Christians and Jews as *dhimmis*, 'peoples of the book'. They could get on with their lives semi-autonomously provided they paid certain special taxes, observed their religious rituals unobtrusively, and generally kept their heads down and learned to accept their second-class but far from intolerable status. A few Christians even prospered by working for the Arab government, sometimes rising to positions of power in the court circles of the rulers in Córdoba, the capital of Muslim Spain.

Learning Arabic, their masters' language, and adopting elements of Arab culture were obvious routes open to collaborationist Christians. But this would only get them so far unless they accepted the ultimate assimilation of converting to Islam. This is precisely what happened, in increasing numbers, in the centuries that followed the Muslim conquest. Tracking this process is extremely difficult with the existing source material. We can be fairly sure that conversion proceeded at different rates among different social levels and in different places: higher status Christians living in towns and in regular contact with Muslim neighbours probably converted faster than lower status country-dwellers, though we cannot know the precise figures. At any rate, by the time that the Christians living in northern Spain began to talk up the idea of holy war in the eleventh and twelfth centuries, constructing an image of themselves in opposition to a well-defined and alien Muslim 'Other', they could do so because the majority of the population in Muslim-controlled Spain were now Muslims, while the Christian communities of the south, hitherto a significant cultural and political bridge between the Christian and Muslim worlds, were shrinking in size and influence. Back in the ninth century, however, this process was still far from complete, and the martyrs movement in the 850s throws light on the tensions and complexities involved at one delicate stage of religious and cultural transition.

The martyrs were a diverse group. Many seem to have been connected to monasteries in the countryside outside Córdoba which cultivated a detached attitude away from the mix of cultures and religions in the hurly-burly of the city. Some of the martyrs were the products of mixed marriages and counted Muslims among their close relatives. A significant number were women. We cannot enter the minds of each individual martyr to probe his or her motivation, but we can be fairly sure that, once the first martyrdoms established a model to follow, they thought of themselves as part of an evolving movement. The typical pattern was for one or more individuals to approach the Muslim authorities and publicly to disparage Islam and the Prophet Mohammed, in the certain knowledge that this was a capital crime in Islamic law. They were, in effect, manoeuvring the authorities into a position where execution was the only possible outcome. We know a good deal about the martyrs, their names, their connections to one another, when and how they died and many other details, thanks to the writings of two of their supporters, Eulogius and Paulus Alvarus.

Eulogius, the more important of the two witnesses, penned several works during the course of the movement, including accounts of how the martyrs met their end, and also letters and treatises defending their actions. Alvarus wrote another treatise in defence of the martyrs, and also an account of Eulogius's life and death (for, appropriately enough, Eulogius himself joined the list of martyrs in 859).

The role of Eulogius in the unfolding events has been much debated. He used to be seen as a central figure in the martyrdom movement, almost its presiding genius. Recently, however, scholars have argued that he was a much more ambiguous figure, closely connected to a few of the martyrs but for the most part a spectator cheering, as it were, from the touchline. Either way, the key point to note about his written output and the work of his follower Alvarus is that it was not about objective description. They were writing polemics, partly directed towards the martyrs' supporters to strengthen their morale and perhaps to encourage more martyrdoms, and partly against critics within the Christian community. It is clear that many Christians, perhaps the majority, disapproved of the martyrs' actions because it upset their delicate relationship with the Muslims. Arguments about the rights and wrongs of the martyrdoms were caught up in wider debates about how the two religions should co-exist, debates that were played out both publicly and, in many instances, privately within religiously divided families. The surviving sources are themselves part of that story and that debate, not detached observations made after the event.

The fact that Eulogius died in 859, the year that the movement is generally considered to have subsided, raises the possibility that there were more martyrdoms, only without Eulogius around to record them. But from what Alvarus tells us, we can be fairly confident that the movement did indeed run out of steam at this time. The years 851–9, therefore, stand out as a discrete phase distinguishable from what precedes and follows it. There are, of course, links to earlier and later times. The tensions that exploded in the 850s may have been building up since the 820s; and there is scattered evidence for a few martyrdoms, apparently uncoordinated but broadly similar to the 850s incidents, around the first third of the tenth century. In themselves, however, these earlier and later phases do not substantially blur the distinctiveness of what happened in the 850s. The challenge therefore becomes what to do with this highly unusual and all-too-brief surge in the depth and range of the information at our disposal. Was Eulogius typical of Christian thinkers around this time, or should we see him as the sort of person who is usually condemned to operate on the fringes of influence and power unless exceptional opportunities bring him or her unexpectedly to the fore? How fully can we reconstruct the ideas of Eulogius's Christian opponents from his bitter condemnations and probable misrepresentations of them? Just how exceptional were the events of 851–9 – a relatively slight racking up of a more or less constant state of tension, or a complete overturning of regular religious and familial relations? To what extent was Córdoba typical of places where Christians and Muslims lived as neighbours? Why were there not more outbursts like the 850s martyrs movement? In short, how far can we push the material that Eulogius and Alvarus wrote beyond its immediate geographical, chronological and socio-cultural setting while still bearing in mind the unusual conditions that created it in the first place?

All the sources that we use are, in their nature, very precisely culturally situated. That is to say, they are products of the specific time and place in which they were created. This is as true of a routine entry in an eleventh-century survey concerning the number of sheep and cows in a farm in Dorset, and a perfunctory three-line writ from the twelfth century commanding a royal official to restore someone's property, as it is of a learned theological treatise by a thirteenth-century academic at the University of Paris, or of a fourteenth-century visionary's account of his or her mystical visions. This might seem like an obvious thing to say, but it is deceptively easy to fudge the issue when it comes to studying different sorts of sources in detail. Medieval sources do not all wear their medieval-ness in the same ways, and this makes it tempting to hunt for sources that scarcely seem to wear their medieval-ness at all. The hope can be that, if only every now and then, someone in the Middle Ages who was writing or making something that we now treat as a source was able to step outside the mental boundaries of his or her contemporaries' world, and to open up a perspective on that world that comes closer to how we imagine we would have seen it ourselves. These supposedly privileged observers become, in effect, time travellers by proxy.

An excellent example of the pitfalls of this approach is provided by *The Murder of Charles the Good* by Galbert of Bruges, a historical narrative born of political crisis. Early one morning in March 1127, Charles, the count of Flanders, was murdered as he prayed in the church of St Donatian next to his castle in Bruges (in what is now northern Belgium). This act stunned public opinion, and it triggered a remarkable sequence of events. First of all, those who sided with the murderers were besieged within Bruges by forces loyal to Charles' memory. Bit by bit they were forced back until, ironically, their last refuge was the very part of the church of St Donatian where Charles had been cut down. Eventually the besieged had to surrender, and a few days later they were put to death by being thrown one by one from the top of a tower. The ringleaders of the conspiracy who had earlier managed to escape were hunted down and killed. This bloody retribution was only the prelude, however, to a more serious and destructive period of civil war. Charles had died without a close male heir, and various aristocratic factions, supported by the kings of England and France who had competing strategic interests in the region, fought for the vacant countship. The situation was only resolved more than a year later, in July 1128, when the main pretender to the comital title, William Clito, died as a result of his wounds, leaving the field unexpectedly clear for his beleaguered rival Thierry of Alsace, who went on to rule Flanders for the next forty years.

Soon after Charles' death, a man named Galbert began to take notes and write up an account of what was happening. Galbert was a middle-ranking official in the count's bureaucracy in Bruges, someone who not only knew many of the main aristocratic protagonists in the drama that was unfolding around him, but also, to a considerable extent, identified with the ordinary people of Bruges and had a sense of Flemish patriotism that went beyond narrow class interest. The disruption of the count's government that must have followed Charles' death gave Galbert an enforced period of leisure, and this is what started him off as a historian; before this point he had not, as far as we know, written history at all. Galbert extended his work as events around him developed. What began as an account of the murder and siege expanded into a history of Charles' rule as count of Flanders, and of the civil war up to Thierry of Alsace's surprise triumph. Galbert's work is a *tour de force*, a gripping, vivid history full of engaging anecdote and human detail. It is available in an excellent English translation by James Bruce Ross (the Introduction to which, incidentally, is, though now dated, one of the very best of its kind). Three things can strike a reader in particular: the fact that Galbert was so close to the events that he describes, many of them happening virtually under his nose; the fact that he was writing so close in time to the events; and his penchant for observational, realistic detail, which makes him an important source for a host of things as varied as the construction of medieval siege-ladders, the layout of the town of Bruges, and the conduct of judicial duels. These qualities would seem to detach Galbert from other twelfth-century historians, none of whose work (with the partial exception of some eye-witness accounts of crusade expeditions) has the same sense of sustained closeness.

If this was where judgements about Galbert ended, there would be no problem. The snag, however, is that until recently scholars have tended to reinvent Galbert as a twelfth-century version of a modern reporter. Not only was he fortunately close to the subject matter of his history, the argument went, he was free of the mental baggage that someone like a monastic chronicler would have brought to the same story. Galbert's very mediocrity, the fact that he was not too educated, not too important, not too stuck in traditional ways of telling stories, liberated him to write a refreshingly candid, uncomplicated account of what he saw and heard. The fact that Galbert's account has a very precise and orderly chronological framework – it is a journalistic text in the literal sense that the action is divided into sequences dealing with separate days – suggested to scholars that they were looking at a piece of raw reporting quite unlike the sort of schematic and distorted version of events that would have been produced by a chronicler chewing over the facts months or years later and interpreting them with the benefit of 20-20 hindsight. Galbert, it had to be admitted, was a lesser light compared to the starriest of the twelfth-century historiographical *galácticos*, but most of his more accomplished history-writing contemporaries were either monks or highly-educated career-clerics, rarified individuals whose backgrounds forced them to see the world around them through twelfth-century cultural lenses. There was something about Galbert, it seemed, which made him more immediate, more real – more like us, in fact.

This is nonsense, of course, and thanks to the work of Jeff Rider and other recent scholars a picture has emerged of Galbert and his work which is much more realistic for being based firmly in early twelfth-century Flanders and the cultural environment in which someone like Galbert must have lived. Careful analysis of Galbert's text is revealing that he was a very sophisticated and thoughtful writer, and what can appear to be straightforward 'journalism' is in fact shot through with contemporary ideas concerning God's role in human affairs, the hierarchical ordering of society, and the workings of justice, amongst other preconceptions. This anchoring in contemporary perspectives is everywhere in the text, and has some interesting implications for what can superficially seem the most straightforward of factual details. It is possible, for example, that Galbert hugely over-simplified the nature and extent of the conspiracy against Charles, because otherwise it would have undermined his pen-portrait of Charles as a broadly, if sometimes begrudgingly, respected ruler whose policies benefited the people of Flanders. Contemporary political thought generally maintained that subjects had a duty to obey even bad rulers, but there was a body of opinion that countenanced resistance against a tyrant in extreme circumstances. Galbert had to prevent his readers from assuming that Charles had brought his downfall upon himself by acting tyrannically, so he pointed the finger of blame very clearly at the members of a single family, the Erembalds, who had risen from humble origins in the service of the counts but had recently become threatened by Charles' attempts to limit their influence over him. Largely thanks to Galbert's description of them, the Erembalds are now firmly established as the villains of the piece. But if the forces that plotted Charles' death were in fact much larger, what would this say about Charles' effectiveness as a ruler? And what would it say about Galbert's manipulation of the facts in order to accommodate contemporary ideals and prejudices? Taking Galbert out of the CNN studio, and putting him back in the streets of Bruges in the 1120s, has the double effect of increasing his interest as an author and of muddying the picture of events to which he contributes. Both of these are signs that we must be doing something right in the ways that we are handling his text as a piece of evidence. We are not, in other words, falling for the illusion of medieval-but-somehow-not-medieval source material serving as a transparent window on the past.

As the case of Galbert clearly illustrates, a great deal of medieval historians' effort is directed towards the reinterpretation of material that is already in the scholarly domain. This is especially true of medieval history before the watershed around 1200, after which the quantity and range of the available source material begin to expand considerably, as we have seen. Before then, when a medievalist says that she or he is doing 'research', this will more often than not involve revisiting well-known sources, many of them available in printed editions (of variable quality) which remove the need to consult the original manuscripts for most routine purposes. This is important to bear in mind because the standard image that the historical profession likes to project is of researchers constantly reinvigorating the subject by hunting down new material in archives and other places. The physical discovery of a new piece of evidence becomes, in effect, a metaphor for the construction of new interpretations of the past. The power of this metaphor is amply demonstrated by the large number of television history documentaries which contrive a plot device such as a newly unearthed diary or a once-secret official dossier in order to blur the distinction between the emotional excitement of historical discovery and the intellectual challenge of historical reinterpretation. The same conflation is also played out very obviously and literally in archaeology documentaries; it is very significant that these are among the most popular forms of television history because they appeal to the sense that the past is not something that exists as a series of interpretations inside people's heads, but is rather something out there waiting to be *found*. It is true that new source material does sometimes come to light; and a great deal of what medieval historians do with their sources is in fact 'new' in the sense that it involves going back to the manuscripts of a text in order to expand upon what can be learned from often old and inaccurate printed editions. But few medieval historians who work on the period before c.1200 can realistically cast themselves as the searchers after new evidence in the same way that an archaeologist will always be hoping to dig up previously unknown physical remains.

Does this mean that the study of medieval history will sooner or later reach saturation point, once every piece of evidence has been identified, carefully edited and thoroughly analyzed? There is perhaps a vague anxiety of this sort hanging over the discipline. Its effect is rather like thinking about the world running out of oil: you know it will happen sometime, but probably later than the doom-mongers say it will, and in the meantime there is no point in getting too worried quite yet. It is an anxiety that has been more directly confronted by scholars in other disciplines with relatively small and seemingly finite source bases, such as classical studies, and it is noteworthy that some branches of medieval studies have begun to follow these other disciplines in searching for coping mechanisms. One such mechanism is to look inwards by accentuating the methodological and technical difficulties of the subject, almost to the point of fetishizing sources as mysteries accessible to a chosen few. Another is to seize on the opportunities offered by Critical Theory to break out of the traditional boundaries within which debate on a particular subject has been conducted, sometimes with very stimulating results, but often not. These trends have been more evident in other branches of medieval studies such as literary criticism and art history than within mainstream history itself, but they are gaining ground there as well. Perhaps in future years they will be seen as the straws in the wind that anticipated a big shift in the nature of the study of medieval history.

But probably not. The point to emphasize is that medieval history as an academic discipline has already been coping and adapting for decades, if not centuries. If there was once a heroic age in which most of the source material still lay undiscovered, that age has long since passed without medieval history grinding to a halt. On the contrary, it has created a niche for itself as a discipline which emphasizes the need to ask new questions of familiar material, and which expands and enriches itself through borrowings from other academic fields. To appreciate this process, it is only necessary to read two examples of, say, a political biography of a medieval king, one written thirty or forty years ago, the other very recently. The footnotes and bibliographies of the two books will contain references to substantially the same body of primary material; it is possible that some new sources have been discovered in the interim, but if so they are more likely to have an influence on specific issues raised within the broader discussion, rather than on the shape of the overall argument itself. In other respects, however, the two books will probably be very different because the questions they ask will differ. It is also likely that the more recent book will draw on secondary (i.e. modern scholarly) works taken from a substantially wider methodological and theoretical range. This would reflect the fact that the boundaries of what constitutes 'history' have become much wider and more permeable.

Medieval history, then, is a subject that prioritizes the search for different questions and is able to renew and refresh itself without always needing the quick fix of locating new source material. In fact the limitations of the source base can be turned into an advantage, because they allow us to make judgements about the relative merits of different historians' analyses of the same body of material. From a medievalist's perspective, debates in modern history can sometimes seem like academic beauty contests in which the reader is invited to prefer one interpretation over another simply on the basis of a gut feeling about what seems the most convincing explanation of events. In equivalent debates in medieval history, it is more likely that a manageable body of core primary material will act as a shared point of reference, making the informed comparison of scholarly views a more feasible and interesting prospect.

It follows that our emphasis must always be on an examination of the sources which is both methodologically rigorous and theoretically open-minded. In saying that, however, it is proper to conclude with a note of due caution. The main problem with any attempt to evaluate the evidence for a slice of the historical past, especially a large and unwieldy slice like the Middle Ages, is that however much one can precisely quantify at least some parts of the surviving source base – by counting the numbers of charters copied into a register, for example, or the number of boxes on an archive shelf – it is never possible to get more than a vague, impressionistic sense of the full and complex relationship between the historical evidence and the vastness of the human experience to which it relates. A good way to illustrate this is to consider the terms in which some specialists in human physiology and psychology, as well as some phenomenological philosophers, have approached the question of how people experience the passing of time moment by moment. One view of our experience of time, and by extension of the things we are doing in it, such as listening to a melody, thinking a thought, or walking down the street, is that it breaks down into a long sequence of individually small units of consciousness. These individual bits of awareness are not simply made up of our immediate sensations at any split-second. They also involve our memory, or retention, of the moment that has just passed, as well as our anticipation, or protention, of the moment that is going to happen immediately afterwards. This three-in-one form of consciousness is what someone reading this sentence will be experiencing....now! It is not a series of random sensations, but the basic building blocks of how we make sense of ourselves and interact with the human and physical world around us: that is to say, how we function as historical actors.

Interestingly, and perhaps a shade conveniently, it has been calculated that this unit of awareness lasts about one second. This allows us to do some straightforward sums about how many of these moments of consciousness a historical actor will get through in a lifetime. Simply for the sake of argument and in the interests of avoiding totals that are unrepresentatively high, we can limit ourselves to an individual's experiences after her or his twelfth birthday (an enormous 'if', in fact, considering the importance of childhood for later life). We can also confine ourselves to this person's waking hours (again, a very big 'if' given the importance that we have learned to attach to people's mental activity during sleep). For someone who dies at the age of 35, which is a reasonable but fairly conservative figure for the average life expectancy of someone in the Middle Ages who survived past childhood, we arrive at a total of about half a billion individual, unique, unrepeatable moments of human consciousness. This, remember, is the accumulated experience of just one person, prince or pauper, queen or maid, scholar or village idiot, who dies fairly young. For most people not one of these moments will ever have made its way into the historical record. And even with respect to the small minority of people who are exceptionally well-served by the surviving evidence, can we presume to say that our evidence relates to anything more than a tiny fraction of everything that they experienced?

All this is, of course, a very crude calculation based on just one theory of temporal perception. But it helps to illustrate the sheer vastness of the past seen as the sum total of human experience, and the sheer inadequacy of the evidence to do anything more than throw some very dim light on the tiniest parts of it. This is perhaps one of the main values of studying the Middle Ages, or indeed any other historical period for which the evidence is thin and uneven. Historians who work on recent history can sometimes become a touch blasé about the capacity of human beings to generate substantial and clear evidence about themselves, but medievalists can never fall for the same mistake. Thinking about the Middle Ages with the source material to hand is hard work; and the imaginative effort that is required to overcome the deficiencies in the evidence is a constant and humbling reminder of the fantastic richness, variety, and complexity of the people and societies that we presume to understand.

4

Is Medieval History Relevant?

What is medieval history actually for? What does it do? Why should we be bothered with it? At one level, the answers to these questions are rooted in the ways that cultures use the past. For individuals and for groups of all sizes the past is a fund of images and stories mobilized to instil a sense of direction and to create and sustain identities. We need the past to anchor ourselves in the present and to project ourselves into hoped-for futures. That is why amnesia and dementia can strike us as so unsettling: encountering someone suffering from severe memory-impairment not only elicits sympathy for a distressing condition, but also prompts reflections on the extent to which personal identity and social interaction hinge on something as apparently banal and taken for granted as the ability to remember.

As far as the medieval period's impact on identities is concerned, while there may well be individuals with some exceptional attachment to this particular part of the past, the chronological separation between then and now means that it is mostly collectivities which draw on the Middle Ages in order to fashion their identities in whole or part. A good example is provided by the modern Lega Nord, a north Italian political movement which exploits the feeling among some northern Italians that their region, which is the most prosperous part of Italy, has to carry the much poorer south. The name is intended to evoke the Lombard Leagues, the associations of northern Italian cities that were formed in the twelfth and thirteenth centuries to resist the German emperors who claimed political control of the region. It might be argued that doing something like borrowing a name from the Middle Ages is just superficial, a sort of loose simile, but the people making these sorts of connections seldom intend something so casual. The nationalist regime of General Franco in Spain, for example, drew extensively on ideas and images inspired by the Spanish Middle Ages – or, more specifically, a vision of the Spanish Middle Ages seen from the point of view of the Christians rather than the Moors or Jews, and of the Castilians more than the other Christians. The official history of the Spanish Civil War (1936–9), which brought Franco to power, was entitled *La Historia de la Cruzada Española* (The History of the Spanish Crusade); it evoked the notion, expressed by Franco himself in a brief quotation set within an illustration that drew heavily on medieval iconography and seamlessly linked the Spanish people of his day with their medieval predecessors, that the civil war was part of a transcendental struggle between civilizations. For medieval Christians defeating Moors, in other words, read twentieth-century Catholic Nationalists defeating irreligious Republicans. And vice versa: in this sort of ideological appropriation, past and present can smoothly morph back and forth.

It should be remembered that the Middle Ages are not the only victim, or culprit, of this sort of theft of the past. One recalls, for example, that Mussolini's Fascist regime in Italy made great play of the memory of classical Rome. The Nazi regime in Germany roamed widely over the past to construct a backstory for its supremacist ideologies. But, as Patrick Geary has pointed out in his stimulating book *The Myth of Nations* (2002), the medieval past is excellent terrain for groups seeking to ground their political or ethnic ambitions in some sort of supposed 'reality': the Middle Ages represent a large enough historical field to offer something for anyone prepared to look hard enough; they are sufficiently distant in time to give modern-day claims rooted in them the authority and prestige of antiquity; but they are not so distant that they must invariably appear too remote from contemporary interests. A central ideological strand of modern Serbian nationalism, for example, which has contributed to recent upheavals in the former Yugoslavia, is the mythology built around a battle which the Serbians fought (and in fact lost) against the Turks in 1389. The extreme right-wing French politician Jean-Marie Le Pen often invokes the early medieval settlement of the Franks in parts of Gaul as the moment when France and Frenchness came into being. The examples could be multiplied many times over. It should not be thought that appropriations of the medieval past are always tendentious at best and sinister at worst. But it would also be unwise to underestimate the ideological charge that can be present within what might seem on the surface to be harmless or neutral representations. Imagine, for example, there is a Western movie that happens to be set in the Middle Ages. For many people in many parts of the world this would be seen not as a bit of escapist fun, but as another example of alien cultural and social values insinuating themselves where they are not wanted.

Trawling through the past in order to reinforce the present is not a modern invention. In the Middle Ages stories were told which linked particular dynasties or peoples back to the distant past. A famous example is the Trojan descent myth of the Franks/French. There were several variants of this story, but in outline it involved a group of refugees fleeing the destruction of Troy by the Greeks, and then gradually migrating westwards. It is debatable whether people in the Middle Ages were expected to believe in the literal truth of such stories or to reflect upon their symbolic value. But the obvious point from our perspective is that the stories are historical nonsense. In contrast, more recent descent myths often wrap themselves in modern scholarly apparatus. For example, the *Ahnenerbe*, the cultural arm of the SS, recruited many distinguished academic historians, ethnologists, archaeologists and other specialists willing to prostitute their researches in the interests of Nazi ideology. As Geary soberly notes, it is the duty of modern-day academic historians to cry out in protest whenever the past is misused, even if no one is particularly willing to listen. The implication of his plea is that the real relevance of medieval history today, if it exists at all, is not to be found in the ways that it can get waylaid by fantasists, ideologues and rogues, but in how it is researched and taught in academic environments. These represent the 'home ground' on which any assessment of the subject's relevance must focus.

This observation seems straightforward enough, but it in fact takes us into an area of heated debate. The status of medieval history as an academic discipline is part of a wider discussion about academic history in general, and here important fault-lines have opened up in recent decades. There are in truth specialists in many beleaguered minority disciplines who would have every reason to envy the prestige and success that history has enjoyed since it became a recognized university discipline in the nineteenth century. There are more people around the world making a livelihood from teaching and researching history, including medieval history, than ever before. So what seems to be the problem? The problem, in fact, is in finding compelling answers to why history, medieval history included, needs to be studied in the first place. There is a school of thought that would answer 'just because': that is to say, history has an intrinsic, almost mystical, interest, and it must be studied for its own sake. There are other voices, however, which insist on a wider social value for academic history. There is a great deal to commend this view: even when professing Olympian disdain for the outside world, academic historians have always traded on their subject's usefulness beyond the university gates. In Britain, for example, when history became established in universities, it soon joined Classics as a subject particularly valued for the way in which it could shape the minds of society's political and cultural elites.

In more recent years, it has become fashionable to ponder what it is about studying history at a high level that benefits its students. What skills and qualities do they gain from it? Is it the ability to weigh up conflicting evidence and synthesize opposing views? The ability to express one's ideas in a clear and organized fashion? The ability to work through a large body of material and discriminate between the relevant and the irrelevant within it? An appreciation of the enormous variety and complexity of human experience? A recognition of the provisional nature of knowledge and a distrust of easy certainties? All of the above? The impetus for asking these sorts of questions has largely come from a re-examination of the role of universities and colleges that teach humanities subject, especially now that only a minority of their graduates go on to pursue careers, such as teaching, which substantively correspond to the subject(s) they learned as students. The modish word for this is 'employability': what does history contribute to the world of employment and, by extension, society at large? Pressured to find answers to this question, many academics would now place a greater emphasis than before on the collateral benefits of studying history: the skills of organization, discrimination and communication that it fosters.

But this comes with a catch, for if the main point of studying history is to acquire collateral skills, does it matter which particular bits of history are studied? The merits of studying, say, ancient Greece, medieval France, eighteenth-century North America or twentieth-century Africa, will reside, not in the actual differences between these bits of the past, but in how well they happen to work as delivery vehicles for the skills of employability. It is easy to see why many historians are uneasy about this 'skills turn' in their subject. Interestingly, too, it is noticeable that some university history departments at least are trying to hold on to the principle that they should offer teaching in a wide chronological and geographical spread of history. In other words, the idea persists that the specifics of *what* students learn matter as least as much as *how* they do it. Otherwise one could just as well imagine a large academic department staffed by people who all specialized in the same narrow area of history, provided only that they taught all the necessary collateral skills.

This is all well and good, and it might be supposed that medieval history stands to benefit from a purist insistence that students should be exposed to a wide range of historical topics. But there is a further catch. For in response to pressures to justify their subject, some historians have chosen to complicate the picture. The weakness of the history-as-skills line of self-justification is that it is very difficult to distinguish meaningfully between history and similar humanities disciplines which operate equally well as ways to encourage organization, intellectual rigour, and clarity of expression. At the margins each subject has skills specific to it, but these are less significant than the large areas of overlap. So why do history at all, when English or Classics or theology or any number of subjects hit the right employability buttons just as well? A response developed by historians working on the more recent past has been to emphasize the relevance of their subject: relevance, that is, understood in the sense of how knowledge of the past directly feeds into an understanding of the present. Medieval history thus stands to lose out because it cannot play the relevance card. Or can it?

Questions about the value of subjects such as medieval history are much more than an opportunity for some bracing academic soul-searching. They also get asked in much more awkward and threatening ways by people who are not on the inside track, people with power like university administrators and politicians. For example, in May 2003 Charles Clarke, the British Secretary of State for Education (that is to say, one of the most senior politicians in the national government and the person in ultimate charge of the British education system from top to bottom), was reported to have said in a speech: 'I don't mind there being some medievalists around for ornamental purposes, but there is no reason for the state to pay them.'[14] Clarke was not the first person to express these sorts of sentiments, and he will not be the last. By looking at what he said, and what others said back, we can begin to think about some of the broader questions that his remarks raise about the point of medieval history.

The main argument of Clarke's speech was that people should be encouraged to study 'useful' subjects at university, which would also mean that resources would be much better spent on academics who teach and research those sorts of subjects than on those who specialize in supposedly useless fields. The notion of usefulness is in fact much more problematic than it at first appears. Useful to whom or what, and in what sorts of ways? But Clarke's thinking, such as it was, is part of a long tradition of judging the merits of educational opportunities in terms of their knock-on effects on the state and on society generally.

We will all be better off, so the argument goes, if people go to university to develop expertise in subjects with an obvious social value, such as medicine, or in those with transparent economic benefits such as business studies, computer sciences and engineering. Needless to say, when the report of Clarke's remarks caused an uproar, there was an attempt by his officials to fudge the issue with 'spin' and claims that he had been misquoted by troublemakers. They actually dug an even deeper hole for themselves by stating that Clarke had been making a comparison between modern educational organizations and medieval universities, which he argued had only taught 'pure' academic subjects that had no wider social impact. This is in fact completely untrue. In any event, the question of what Clarke actually said or meant to say is less significant than the fact that the reporting of his alleged remarks created so much unease. Clarke had touched a raw nerve. However much we want it to, does all this medieval history really add up to anything of substance? Or is it just a bit of decorative ornamentation?

The counterattacks by medievalists were robust. Some attacked Clarke himself as a philistine thug, which was good, rousing stuff but did not get to the root of the problem. The bigger issue was that the furore was not about one individual's unsophisticated thinking and confrontational manner; Clarke was expressing ideas which have been bubbling away in political and educational debate for some time, and in many places besides Britain. Moreover, as Clarke the successful politician would well know, there are not many votes in being a champion of medieval history and other 'ornamental' disciplines, whereas the notion that universities and colleges are in some way refuges for too many people doing too many 'useless' subjects at other people's expense is a prejudice that can readily be sold to many members of the general public.

Some of the responses to Clarke attacked his position on his own chosen ground by pointing out that the past is itself a resource with social and economic dimensions. In a country such as Britain, the argument runs, the tourism and heritage industries employ large numbers of people, encouraging investment and earning large amounts of foreign currency. As the people at the sharp end of society's efforts to find out and interpret the past, historians, medievalists included, should be seen as an important part of this economic structure. They help to energize the system by providing the stimulus of new ideas, which then spread out through their teaching and in the popularization of their research. That at least is the ideal. In reality, one has to wonder to what extent cutting-edge academic history actually affects the ways in which the past is packaged and sold by the tourism industry. There are connections, but they are not always straightforward nor necessarily consistent. And what about places such as North America where there are medieval historians but no medieval tourist sites? Even up-scale and serious-minded packagings of the past – the sorts of thing that one comes across in scholar-friendly places like museums and historic buildings – tend to draw on some parts of academic history's disciplinary range much more than on others. There is generally more call for political history, art history and architectural history, for example, than for intellectual history, cliometrics (the use of statistical methods in historical enquiry) or diplomatic (the technical study of documents). Overall then, this line of argument against the Clarke position is good as far as it goes because it erodes a key assumption underpinning the anti-medievalist position: that so-called 'useless' subjects and the 'real world' never get to meet. But it works better for some historical subjects and methodologies than for others, so it fails as a justification for medieval history across the board.

Another counter to Clarke's attack on the value of medieval history was to take the moral high ground. Clarke's ideas were misconceived, the argument went, because they were too narrowly utilitarian, falsely equating the value of something with its tangible and visible benefits. The benefits of studying the Middle Ages are in reality intangible, said Clarke's critics: like all humanities subjects, the fact that medieval history is researched and taught contributes to our level of civilization and encourages many of the values that we like to think are prized in our cultural tradition – values such as tolerance, open-mindedness, a willingness to challenge traditional ideas, and an appreciation of human potential in all its diversity. Medieval history is, in short, part of our collective soul. To be honest, this connection can often seem rather airy-fairy, more a pious hope than a phenomenon with clearly observable effects. Supporters of the Clarke view would doubtless argue that when medieval historians argue in these terms, this is a case of professional self-interest passing itself off as high-minded public service. But it would be wrong to be quite so cynical. To a greater or lesser extent every practising medievalist signs up to this belief and hopes that this comes across in his or her research and teaching. If there is a problem, it is that this argument only works well on a fairly abstract, impressionistic level. It would be impossible (not to say wholly inappropriate!) to go out into the street, point accusing fingers at specific individuals, and pronounce that their lives are the poorer for lack of an education in medieval history, or history in general, or any humanities subject for that matter. So the medieval-history-does-us-good argument has both intellectual and emotional force, a combination that means that it should be taken especially seriously, but it can only be an incomplete defence against the attacks of the Clarkist philistines.

As the responses to Charles Clarke reveal, much of the case for medieval history is that it stands or falls with all the other potentially vulnerable subjects such as Classics (another one on Clarke's hit list) and philosophy (which would in fact be spared his axe). There is a sense in which there is safety in numbers. More broadly still, questions about the value of academic subjects like medieval history are part of a wider debate about the place in modern society of art and culture. This debate has been running for centuries, and contributions to it made a long time ago can still possess a very modern resonance. Consider, for example, Victor Hugo's battle cry against the demolishers of medieval buildings in an article written in 1832. Hugo (1802–85), best known today as the author of *Les Misérables* (1862), was a keen medievalist in the early part of his writing career. As we saw in Chapter 1, the most famous demonstration of this interest is his novel *Notre-Dame de Paris* (1831), which reveals a fascination with medieval architecture that Hugo also expressed in public life. He served on committees dedicated to the preservation of France's architectural heritage, and thundered in print against the local government officials, architects and business interests who were tearing down old buildings all over France in the name of progress or profit. Returning to the theme of an article that he had penned in 1825, 'War on the Demolishers!', Hugo's 1832 essay pilloried what he saw as the barbarism, ignorance, brutality and vandalism behind the demolition of old monuments. Every day an ancient memory of France was being lost along with the stones on which this memory had been inscribed. This was like an old book of venerable traditions being torn up page by page. 'Since when,' Hugo asked, 'have people in a fully civilized society dared to ask of art what is its utility? Woe betide you if you don't know what art is for! There isn't anything more we can say to you. Go on, then! Demolish! Utilize!'[15] Charles Clarke, please note.

In recent decades there has also been another sort of challenge to medieval history, a challenge that has been more precisely targeted and is for that reason even more serious. This comes from within the discipline of history itself, specifically from historians working on later periods who wonder whether medieval history is relevant. 'Relevant' is every bit as slippery a category as 'useful', one of the reasons why an accusation of irrelevance can be so difficult to shake off entirely. But in essence the modernist argument is that medieval history is simply too far back in time to provide helpful examples of the ways in which our past and our present interconnect. The obvious retort here is that the reasons for studying history are not just to do with explaining today's world in a mechanistic X-caused-Y sort of way, as even historians of the very recent past would have to concede. Thinking about chains of cause and effect is what lay people usually imagine historians do, but historical understanding is in fact much more layered and subtle. That said, it is unavoidably the case that modern history possesses a different edge because it throws up so many links to our own experience. When asked to develop an understanding of the fall of the Berlin Wall, for example, one could profitably go back into the nineteenth century and the unification of Germany under Bismarck, whereas it would be far more of a stretch to factor in the emergence of the East Frankish kingdom, the forerunner of Germany, way back in the ninth century. At best ninth-century origins would have a place, but only as general 'background' or 'context', whereas more recent events and processes could be accorded a much more hard-edged quality as 'reasons', 'causes', 'major factors' and so on. The logic of the irrelevance argument, of course, is that at some unspecified point between yesterday and the end of the Middle Ages there is a line beyond which relevance fades into nothingness. Where this line might actually lie is, naturally, left open, but medievalists can at least be confident that they are on the wrong side of it!

Allied to this has been the criticism of medieval history along the lines that it is a relic of an old-fashioned, Eurocentric historical vision. In other words, medieval history developed as an academic discipline from the nineteenth century onwards because it neatly slotted somewhere in the middle of a 'grand narrative' which privileged the story of powerful, Western, white males at the expense of the histories of other groups and civilizations. Even the most cursory survey of the topics that medievalists work on nowadays reveals immediately that, if there ever was a time when this characterization of medieval history had some real basis, that time is long gone. But mud sticks. The result is that to the charge of irrelevance by reason of chronological remoteness is added the crime of aiding and abetting ideological conservatism.

The issue of relevance is very real. Whether or not it is mentioned openly, relevance influences the choices that people make about what they study, the books that publishers decide to publish, the jobs that colleges and universities try to fill, and the places that people like Charles Clarke put their money. So it is not pandering to philistines' attacks and modernists' jibes to think about medieval history in these terms. It is not wrong to be defensive, as long as we remember to build outwards from defence towards identifying positive arguments in favour of the importance of medieval history as an academic discipline. What, then, is so relevant about medieval history? Rather than get lost in a mass of generalizations right at the start, it might be helpful to begin our discussion by focusing on one example of how things that happened in the Middle Ages still affect us today. This is the English language. Language pervades our day-to-day, indeed our moment-by-moment, experience. In this respect it is perhaps unique. In most situations our exposure to the remnants of the past, in particular the more distant past, tends to be uneven and variable. Some people, for example, live in places 'rich in history', as the tourist blurb might say, but most of us do not. The inclination to visit historic sites or to read history books varies from individual to individual. On the other hand, language is everywhere and affects virtually everyone. It is something that we acquire in the normal scheme of things without worrying unduly, if at all, about its antecedents – without, that is, making a conscious decision to think historically.

But is something like a language a real part of history? As a subject in schools and universities, the development of English traditionally features in linguistic and literary curricula more than in the teaching of 'mainstream' history. This is, however, nothing more than a matter of academic convention dating back to the mapping out of subjects' boundaries when school and university education expanded in the nineteenth and twentieth centuries. Language is a key part of how individuals and groups function culturally, socially, politically and ideologically, and this makes it a proper subject of historical enquiry. More than this, language can itself provide evidence for many historical processes which had effects far beyond the specifically linguistic domain, for example shifts in social patterns, political upheavals, technological developments, educational reform, mass migrations and colonial encounters between different peoples. A great deal of history, in other words, has left its mark on our language.

If we go back to the roots of today's English – or, to be more accurate, the different Englishes used around the world – we find that the Middle Ages were an important and formative period. Conventionally (we shall be looking at the limitations of the convention later) the story of English is said to begin with the arrival in Britain, in the fifth and sixth centuries, of members of some of the Germanic tribes that lived on or near the coast of what is now the northern Netherlands, north-west

Germany and southern Denmark. The classic statement of what happened is that made by the great Anglo-Saxon historian Bede, writing in the eighth century:

> They came from three very powerful Germanic tribes, the Saxons, Angles, and Jutes. The people of Kent and the inhabitants of the Isle of Wight are of Jutish origin and also those opposite the Isle of Wight...From the Saxon country, that is, the district now known as Old Saxony, came the East Saxons, the South Saxons, and the West Saxons. Besides this, from the country of the Angles...came the East Angles, the Middle Angles, the Mercians, and all the Northumbrian race (that is those people who dwell north of the river Humber) as well as the other Anglian tribes.[16]

Bede's scheme has its problems. Historians debate the true importance of the Jutes, for example, and it is likely that other groups not mentioned by Bede also took part in the broad migration. Nonetheless, scholars would agree with Bede about the significance of the Angles and Saxons, who between them took over most of the area of modern-day England. The migrants did not all speak one uniform language, but the many similarities between their dialects were such that we can classify them as a single language community. In due course *Englisc* became the most common name for the speech of Angles and Saxons alike.

English is part of what philologists call the West Germanic group of languages, which also includes Dutch and German. The language in this group which is closest to English is Frisian. This is English's one 'sister' (to use the helpful but slightly old-fashioned system of expressing the links between languages in terms of family relationships). Frisian, which today is never its speaker's sole language, exists in two variant forms: one, spoken in small pockets around the south-western corner of the Jutland peninsula, has all but died out; the other, found in parts of the northern Netherlands, has benefited from recent official support after years of suppression and now numbers about 300,000 speakers. It is interesting to reflect that the fates of the two 'sisters' have been so different: one has become a global language spoken by hundreds of millions and understood by millions more, the other survives as a minority language whose speakers can be numbered in a few hundreds of thousands. But the affinity is striking. It is often expressed in a well-worn ditty which can be traced back to the eighteenth century and is now greeted with slightly weary amusement by Frisian-speakers: 'Butter, bread and green cheese / Make good English and good Frise'.

The speech of the Anglo-Saxons, nowadays termed 'Old English', has supplied the main grammatical structure and the core vocabulary, or base 'register', of modern English. A good way to think about our debt to Old English is to imagine someone stranded on a desert island and forced to lead a very simple existence. Words that express the basic features of our castaway's world and the ways in which he or she functions in it are predominantly Anglo-Saxon in origin: for example *day, night, heat, sun, fire, rain, cold, hunger, thirst, eat, food, drink, water, tears, laughter, see, think, find, feel, hope, dream, live.* On the other hand, if matters had simply continued to stand as they were after the Anglo-Saxon settlement in Britain, modern English would be very different from how we know it today. In particular it would feel much more obviously and exclusively part of the West Germanic language family. Yet as anyone who learns other European languages, living or dead, soon realizes, it is a peculiarity of modern English that it seems to have a great deal in common with many other languages without being really close to any of them – close, that is, in the way that speakers of Norwegian and Swedish or of Spanish and Portuguese can normally communicate with one another quite easily even if they have no formal training in the other language. This characteristic of semi-detachment is a result of the fact that the Old English core of our language has been added to by many subsequent developments, the most important of which took place during or very soon after the medieval period.

The first significant change was the introduction of Old Norse by Danish and, to a lesser extent, Norwegian settlers in many parts of northern and eastern England between the ninth and eleventh centuries. The newcomers' language was part of the Germanic family and therefore related to English; in many instances the modern form of a word would be the same if it were descended from English or Norse. It is unlikely that an Anglo-Saxon and a Dane coming face to face for the first time would have immediately been able to strike up a conversation. But if they lived in neighbouring villages, their communities would have gradually developed the ability to understand one another, exploiting affinities between their two languages and borrowing words from each other until something like a single hybrid language emerged. This is significant because the later medieval regional dialect from which modern standard English is descended was that spoken in the eastern-central part of England. This included areas where Norse-speakers had once settled in significant numbers, but also places, including London, where their influence had been slight. The result was that this 'East Midland' dialect showed the clear influence of Norse without being dominated by it. If modern English had come to be based on dialects spoken further south and west, where there was no Danish migration to speak of, we would nowadays expect it to have retained more pure Old English features; if derived from dialects spoken further north, where the Norse settlement was concentrated, it would now have a more pronounced Scandinavian feel. The overall contribution of Norse to our current word-pool is quite small, though it equips our castaway with several basic words such as *cut, die, dirt, egg, get, happy, hit, ill, knife, skin, sky, take, want* and *weak*. In some respects, however, the influence runs very deep: the verb 'to be' and the personal pronouns are among the inner bastions of most languages, so it is noteworthy that the words *are, they, them* and *their* come from Norse.

The interactions between speakers of Old English and Norse broadly involved two communities with similar social patterns and cultural traditions, especially once the Viking settlers converted to Christianity. In the early decades of the eleventh century there was a period when Scandinavians occupied the throne of England and made up a large part of the kingdom's aristocratic elite. But this was not a decisive factor in the long-term impact of Scandinavian speech on the English language. This forms a noteworthy contrast with the next major influence on English, the French speech and cultural values brought to England with the Norman Conquest. In the aftermath of William the Conquerors's decisive defeat of King Harold at Hastings in 1066, and especially once Old English was jettisoned as a language of government soon thereafter, French became the language of a small but politically and economically dominant elite. The elimination of many members of the Anglo-Saxon ruling classes, and the social degradation of most of those who survived, meant that English was squeezed out as a language of power and prestige. In the process it became more exclusively associated with the world of lower-status people, that is to say precisely the same sorts of peasants, artisans, humbler townspeople and servants who had already accounted for the great majority of English-speakers before 1066. French retained its superior status for about three centuries. Exchanges between francophone masters and their anglophone subordinates occurred in a wide variety of situations over a long period of time. This meant that the influence of French upon English was complex and layered. In fact to speak of the influence of 'French' in the singular is misleading, for there were successive influences, first the Norman French dialect that came with the conquerors, and then the central French dialect which from the twelfth century onwards became the high-prestige international language of literature, courtliness and chivalry. This double effect explains several dual borrowings into English from the same French root, for example *warranty/guarantee, warden/guardian* and *catch/chase*.

There is a well-known scene near the beginning of *Ivanhoe* in which the two principal lower-status characters, Gurth and Wamba, who are of course Anglo-Saxons, ponder the impact of the Norman Conquest as it had become reflected in the words used for farmyard animals. Saxon peasants tend the animals when they are alive, French masters eat them once they are cooked: hence couplets such as *swine/pork, ox/beef, calve* (calf)/*veau* (veal). This passage has become so well known that it is sometimes easy to overlook the fact that it is not a primary source. But Walter Scott had indeed spotted something important about the differences between Anglo-Norse and French words within the language. Just keeping to his example of live and cooked animals, his list could be extended to include the pairings *sheep/mutton, deer/venison* and *fowl/poultry*. More broadly, one finds many examples of differences in nuance and degree of formality expressed in pairs of words such as *begin/commence, book/volume, pretty/beautiful, hearty/cordial,* and *hide/ conceal*. In modern English, French loan-words predominate in areas such as government, the arts and the law (though *law* itself is from Old Norse). On the other hand, it would be wrong to imagine the impact of French as nothing more than a linguistic makeover helping simple Anglo-Norse peasants to become more cultured and refined. As anyone who has worked through long lists of French vocab at school will attest, there have been numerous borrowings from French into English in all aspects of our lives. Even our desert-island castaway leading his or her low-register existence will benefit from *air, safety, fresh fruit, prey* to *catch*, a *message* in a *bottle* and, when help eventually arrives, a *voice* to *cry* out with.

An important by-product of the Norman Conquest was that it reasserted the special status of Latin as the language of the Church and of learning. Pre-Conquest England had been unusual in that the native language, or at least a high literary form of it, had enjoyed the sort of prestige that was reserved for Latin elsewhere in western Europe. The Old English *Anglo-Saxon Chronicle*, for example, our single most important source for events in pre-Conquest England, has no contemporary parallel on the European mainland. It is true that Latin had been influential in England before the arrival of the Normans, and this had had some impact on the English language. Earlier still, in fact, as a result of contacts between the Romans and their northern barbarian neighbours across the Rhine frontier, there had already been borrowings from

Latin into West Germanic before the Anglo-Saxon migration: these include the homely 'butter' and 'cheese' of our Anglo-Frisian ditty. Latin's impact on English after 1066, however, was immeasurably greater, in large part because it was reinforced by the influence of French, which is itself descended from Latin. Sometimes it is difficult to tell whether a word with a Latin root in modern English has come direct from the Latin itself or indirectly via French. As the language of education and learning, however, Latin has generally not needed to be mediated by French to make an enormous impact on those parts of our vocabulary which express technical and abstract concepts. In this it has been joined by Greek, whose influence on English began to be felt in the sixteenth century with the revival of the study of that language during the Renaissance. Countless of our modern technical, scientific and cultural terms are compounds of elements derived from one or both of these two languages.

This has interesting results which illustrate how the historical dimension can feed through into contemporary usage and perceptions. Unlike the other Germanic languages, which typically create complex words by drawing on their own basic lexical resources (as did Old English), modern English tends to change register from the everyday and informal to the more formal and abstract by means of a shift from Anglo-Norse to Latin and Greek, with French moving back and forth somewhere in the middle. Parents of inquisitive children will recognize how being asked to explain an unfamiliar word often involves a straightforward transliteration of the word's classical roots into their simpler English equivalents. What does 'translucent' mean? – lets light through. 'Hydrophobia'? – fear of water. The list is endless. A bright Frisian-speaking child coming across the word *wintersliep* for the first time should be able to work out what it means from first principles; an English-speaking child confronted with *hibernation* will not, unless he or she already happens to know that *hiber* is the Latin for 'winter'. It is not entirely fanciful to suppose that the presence within English of vocabulary registers with different roots has important, if largely subconscious, effects on people's reactions to one another. The use of higher-register words taken from Latin and Greek tends to be more pronounced within the discourses of specialist professions such as medicine, science, the law and academia. This may well influence the attitudes of incomprehension, suspicion, deference or disregard that tend to be shown towards these activities by members of the general public.

Overall, then, we can see that the Middle Ages were the time of various important stages in the development of the English language. This permits us to conclude that here is a clear case of the study of medieval history being potentially 'relevant', in the sense that it furthers our understanding of a significant aspect of our present-day experience. On the other hand, the example of English also helps us to identify countervailing arguments which sound notes of due caution. These cautions are, moreover, valid well beyond the specific example that we have been considering, and have a much wider bearing on the relevance of medieval history as a whole.

The first and most fundamental issue involves the question of narrativity, that is to say how we turn things into stories. The above sketch of the history of English has deliberately used loaded terms such as 'story' and 'development' in order to create a sense of movement through time. Different events and processes were arranged according to a structural framework that allocates an appropriate place for everything that happened. Like any story that makes basic sense, the outline sketch had a beginning (the arrival of the Anglo-Saxons in Britain), a middle (various subsequent influences on English, described in chronological order), and an end (the stage reached by English by the sixteenth century). The stages are made to run together in a cumulative way. As far as people on the ground at the time were concerned, many episodes that form part of the story, like the arrival of the Vikings or the Norman Conquest, must have felt like major upheavals and clear breaks from past experience. But we are in a position to stand back and take the longer view, and this equips us to finesse all the short-term discontinuities in the interests of smoothing out the bigger story. According to this approach, there *is* a story about English to be told because there *was* a story-like structure to the way in which events unfolded. In other words, a narrative chain exists which links some fifth-century Anglo-Saxons jumping from the bows of their boats onto a beach somewhere in southern or eastern Britain, to Shakespeare penning his latest play more than eleven centuries later. By extension, we can imagine that the story-structure did not stop with Shakespeare, but has continued up to our own day. Consequently everything that forms part of the story is, by definition, 'relevant' because it has a place in the unbroken narrative structure that we use to make sense of the whole – a whole that extends up to the present.

To a greater or lesser extent, most of the history that we read is supported by a narrative structure of some sort. This is not only true of histories in which the element of story-telling is clearly visible on the surface of what we read, such as a biography or an account of a particular episode like a battle. It also underpins other forms of presenting historical argument: even a graph or column of figures, for example, will only make sense if related to a narrative of change or continuity over time. The question of narration in history, however, has been hotly debated in recent decades. The critics of traditional history-writing's reliance on narration have launched their attacks from two directions. The past itself does not come neatly packaged in story form, they argue, because the reality of lived experience is that it is shapeless, bitty and chaotic. And in any event, so it is claimed, historians impose narrative structure on the past, not as objective seekers after 'how it really was', but in order to pursue their own ideological agendas.

This is not the place to go into these debates in detail, but a few general remarks are helpful with regard to the first of these criticisms. Defenders of the more traditional view have made a good case for arguing that life really does have an in-built narrative dimension at some basic level. That is to say, the ways in which our minds experience time, when conjoined with our ability to remember past experiences and to anticipate future events, help us to get through the day living a type of story. Each day's story then builds up into a bigger story over time: we do not have to reinvent ourselves when we wake up every morning. The notion that an individual experiences life as a form of story can reasonably be extended outwards to apply to small and coherent communities such as a nuclear family or the inhabitants of a village. But even here the strain of imposing a single story on the lives of different people begins to show, and this problem grows as the size of the communities that we are considering expands. When we reach something as large and amorphous as a language community, even as it existed in just one point in time, the story that we are able to tell has to become very schematic in order to be both manageably succinct and reasonably inclusive, for we cannot write certain people out just because they happen to complicate the picture. In our efforts to be schematic and succinct, it is deceptively easy to construct connections through time that do not in fact stand up to close scrutiny. Yet without these sorts of connections, relevance simply cannot function.

A further catch is that when we come to ponder the medieval roots of a modern phenomenon, it is easy to exaggerate the uniquely medieval quality of what we are seeing. The 'story' of English is unusual in that it can be worked into a chronological framework that happens to harmonize with the traditional boundaries of the Middle Ages. The Anglo-Saxons arrived in Britain as the Roman Empire in the West was breaking down; indeed, their migration was one symptom of that larger process. And the transition from 'Middle' to 'Modern' English is

conventionally situated around 1500. It is a neat fit, but it is important
to remember that appearances can be deceptive. When the Anglo-
Saxons put the width of the North Sea between themselves and the
people who spoke similar dialects on the Continent, they were doing
something quite unusual from a linguistic point of view by presenting
us with an artificially clean-looking break. We sometimes visualize the
relationships between languages as connecting lines on a family tree,
with different branches splitting off from one another. But this is just
convenient visual shorthand, not a metaphor meant to suggest how
languages actually evolve. Related languages often stay in contact and
continue to pass influences back and forth unless there are compelling
geographical factors limiting contact between them. The Anglo-Saxons
in Britain entered into a state of relative isolation which created a sort
of linguistic 'laboratory', a space within which, even without the later
influences from Norse, French, Latin and other languages, the grammar
and vocabulary of English would have gradually shifted away from the
other West Germanic languages, in some instances developing new
forms and in others retaining old features which the related continen-
tal languages have subsequently lost.

The fact that this break happened around the start of the medieval
period is no more than a neutral chronological detail which in itself has
no underlying significance. The Germanic languages had a long history before c.400; it is simply that we have virtually no direct evidence of
what they were like (and in any event we have to wait another three
hundred years or so before we find substantial evidence for English).
Nor did the Anglo-Saxons' linguistic isolation necessarily mean that
change had to be rapid. In the eighth century, for example, the conversion to Christianity of parts of what are now Holland and north-
west Germany was spearheaded by Anglo-Saxon missionaries, part of
whose success must have been down to the fact that their native tongue
helped them to pick up the local dialects of the people to whom they
were preaching. It is likely that even towards the end of the Anglo-
Saxon period, Frisian merchants trading in England would have been
able to make themselves understood pretty easily. As late as the
fifteenth century observers were arguing that English was only now
beginning to feel distinct from its Germanic relatives.

The development of other European languages followed different
chronologies, which demonstrates how the superficial medieval-ness of
English's origins has no deep significance. The best examples are the
Romance languages descended from Latin such as French, Italian,
Spanish, Portuguese, and Romanian. These languages were the result of

a long mutation. Latin did not suddenly stop with the end of Roman rule in western Europe. As we have seen, it remained the language of learning and the Church, but just as importantly it continued as the everyday speech of millions of people in most of the areas where the Romans had ruled. Their language changed year by year and generation by generation, shedding many of the more intricate features of Latin grammar and changing the word order in sentences and the pronunciations of words. But this was a slow process and one more evident in some places than others. Language historians place the end of non-educated Latin speech and the emergence of the Romance vernaculars around 600–800, but even such a broad span of time is potentially misleading as a definitive cut-off point. As late as the ninth and tenth centuries, if not later still, educated observers were wrestling with the question of the status of vernacular speech which they could easily hear was related to Latin in some way. Was it just 'bad' Latin or something qualitatively different? If we look at the process of mutation from the other end, we similarly find that the transition from Latin to Romance does not map neatly onto the supposed transition from the Roman to the medieval world. When Cicero (106–43 BC) and Tacitus (c.55–c.117 AD) were writing their finely crafted Latin, they were not using the everyday speech of people in the streets and fields. As the Romans exported Latin to the various parts of their empire, it interacted in a host of subtly different ways with the vocabulary, speech-patterns, grammatical conventions and pronunciations of local languages. The roots of the differences between the modern Romance languages thus lie in this pre-medieval period as well as later. Not all European languages, then, come neatly stamped 'Made in the Middle Ages'.

Another moral to be learned from the history of the English language is that whenever one feels emboldened to identify a strand of relevance connecting the Middle Ages to today, one must be very careful to keep the argument within reasonable and narrow limits. Otherwise the results can be misleading or worse. English is a good illustration of this problem because we seldom think of a language in a narrowly technical sense as a system of sounds and structural rules. It tends to be associated in our minds with wider issues to do with communication, identity, status, and the membership of collectivities. Many people today treat the language(s) they speak as a defining element of their cultural or political identity: the aims of Basque separatists fighting for independence from the Spanish state, for example, are a mix of conventional political objectives and an expression of cultural self-assertion built around the distinctiveness of their language.

So, by analogy to our modern experience, it is reasonable to ask how important language was in the ways that medieval people constructed their identities. But here we encounter a problem to do with the built-in imbalances in the surviving evidence, along the lines of those that we discussed in Chapter 3. Taking the example of English, it is clear that the evidence for the language itself is relatively abundant. Every text in one of the medieval varieties of English bears witness to the history of the language, whatever each text is actually about. It could be a poem, a prose chronicle, a homily, a charter or anything else that happens to survive. But it is likely that the contents of only a small proportion of the surviving body of material will bear directly on other questions that might interest us, such as what, if anything, Englishness meant in the Middle Ages. The temptation then becomes to run the two things together, so that the topic with the thinner evidence expands into the space occupied by the topic about which we have much more information.

In fact, although people in the Middle Ages were sometimes conscious of language as a source of identity, and in some contexts elevated its status to one of the key things that marked one group of people off from another, on the whole they attached less significance to it than we do today. In any event, there was seldom any sort of neat fit between linguistic and political or cultural boundaries. The case of 'English' Scotland is a good illustration. In the Middle Ages, the south-eastern part of Scotland was substantially English-speaking, a situation which dated back to Angle settlement in the region in the early medieval period. When the kingdom of Scotland took shape in the central Middle Ages, this area, Lothian, became an integral part of it. In other words, there is no sense in which this was really a part of England that had somehow got away. Even today many people in Scotland are sensitive to the idea that modern Scots English should be regarded as a discrete linguistic entity which is historically distinct from English English and not a mere outgrowth of it. Similarly, medieval England presents a complex picture. Twelfth-century England in particular enjoyed a lively literary culture even as English itself was losing its prestige. Some of the most important Latin writers in the so-called 'Twelfth-Century Renaissance' were from England or had connections to it. A writer called Geffrei Gaimar wrote a long vernacular history of the English – in French! Many of the patrons of fashionable French literature were English. Clearly, then, any attempt to extrapolate an understanding of medieval English identity from an analysis of the English language itself will run into enormous difficulties.

Thinking about the relevance of the Middle Ages to the English language is also a useful reminder of how much history has happened since c.1500, and of the value of keeping a proper sense of scale. In 1500 English amounted to a group of dialects spoken by probably fewer than 3 million people (the population had in fact been in decline in the fourteenth and fifteenth centuries because of the cumulative effects of plagues and famines). The language was confined to the British Isles, and was only one of the languages spoken in various parts of those islands. English, it is true, was the main language of the single most populous and powerful political entity in the British Isles, but it had not yet achieved universal dominance even within this fairly small area. By 2000, however, English had become a truly global phenomenon. It is the first language of about 350 million people, and is understood and used to a high standard by about as many again. It has been estimated that about 1000 million people around the world are learning English at some or other level.

We tend to think of English as a homogenous thing: the standard forms of the language used in, say, Britain, the United States and Australia are easily mutually intelligible, having diverged less than, for example, Dutch and Afrikaans or French and Canadian French. The effect of mass media and global communications has been to slow down, and in fact reverse, any drifting apart. But it is important not to lose sight of the enormous variety that the spread of English has entailed, as revealed by the large numbers of dialects, creoles and pidgins spoken around the world, as well as by the many applications that the language has found in countries such as India where it enjoys official or quasi-official status. Clearly this extraordinary expansion and diversification have many complex causes which in different ways relate to the growth of first British and then American world power. The point to stress is that these developments cannot be seen as a straightforward, linear extrapolation of the situation that English found itself in around 1500. A great deal of very big history has had to happen since to get us from then to now: technological and scientific transformations, industrialization, imperial expansion, enormous demographic change, Atlantic slavery, political upheavals, and a host of other factors. If we want to regard medieval English as relevant to our modern experience, therefore, we need to acknowledge the profound transformations that characterize the intervening half-millennium. And what is true of English applies equally well to all aspects of medieval life.

It is clear that focusing upon the historical roots of a modern phenomenon can also distort our understanding of its true significance. A good illustration of this is suggested by the modern-day workings of common law, which has its roots in medieval English jurisprudence and nowadays forms the basis of many legal systems around the world, including in the United States. Imagine that two legal cases are being tried in adjacent courts. In one, the case concerns a crime or tort (civil wrong) that has, in various guises, been part of the common law tradition as far back as the Middle Ages. In the other, the defendant is being prosecuted or sued under the terms of a statute that was only enacted a year before, and relates to circumstances which are in their nature recent – say, internet fraud. In one sense the experience of the two trials will be very different according to their different historical reaches. The former case will be discussed and judged with reference to the records of similar cases from the past, a back-catalogue of precedents that potentially stretches back to the Middle Ages (though in practice the chronological reach of case-law precedent seldom extends further back than the nineteenth century). The latter case will have no such body of precedent to govern it, at least not directly. If anything, this court will be conscious that its task is to set a precedent: it will be making history, in effect, rather than being constrained to follow it. But from the point of view of the defendants in the two courts, it will probably matter very little whether the law that threatens to punish them is old or new. It is the present state of the law, and its future effects on them, that count. Similarly, from the point of view of the state that makes and enforces laws, a law remains valid, not as an act of homage to the past, but to the extent that it functions effectively in the present and can realistically be expected to influence people's behaviour in the future.

Presentism, the idea that what is happening right now is our only true concern, is naturally anathema to historians, because it seems to undermine the very value of studying the past. But it must be said that presentism is what makes the world turn. On a given day only a tiny fraction of the billions of utterances made in English around the world are consciously informed by a knowledge of the language's history, but people get by just the same. If all the evidence for the history of English were to miraculously disappear overnight, we would still be speaking to one another in the morning. Developing an awareness of something's historical antecedents is never wasted effort and can be very enriching, but in many situations a little relevance goes a long way. Otherwise, to insist too strongly on connections between the past and the present is to confuse a phenomenon's *causes*, which are of course historical, and its *meaning*, which is largely determined by our reactions to the circumstances in which we find ourselves in the present.

Sometimes even a little relevance can be too much. An excellent example comes in the form of the crusades, which, as we shall see, have been corralled into contemporary debates that are prompted by current affairs. Before we consider the modern dimension, however, it is important to gain a clear historical perspective. So, what was a crusade? This question has been the subject of heated scholarly discussion in recent years, a debate in part fuelled by the fact that the terminology that medieval people themselves used to describe crusading was often allusive or euphemistic. The best modern definition, and the most influential, has been that devised by the leading crusade historian Jonathan Riley-Smith. In Riley-Smith's formulation the key defining elements of a crusade are, first, that it was a war authorized and proclaimed by the pope acting as Christ's mouthpiece, rather than a secular ruler such as an emperor or king. Second, the war had a pronounced penitential quality, that is to say the participants were meant to believe that their actions would undo the consequences of some or all of the sins that they had committed. Third, the participants took a vow, a formal religious promise like that taken by pilgrims; this committed them to the enterprise and was formally marked by their wearing a cross on their clothes. A crusade was also fought for what was believed to be a just cause, such as the defence of other Christians or the recovery of Christian territory, and this cause was in theory conceived as in the interests of the whole Church, not just the area immediately affected by the crusade. The effect of this definition is that it simultaneously broadens and narrows our range of reference relative to the impressionistic and imprecise ways in which the word 'crusade' is often used.

It broadens our understanding because it is clear that this definition continues to be valid for situations well beyond the traditional cut-off point for crusade history of 1291, the year in which the last vestige of the western European control of parts of Syria and Palestine that had begun with the First Crusade (1095–1101) came to an end. Most scholars nowadays would push the history of crusading into the sixteenth century and even beyond: over such an extended period, crusading of course mutated into different forms, but there is an underlying continuity which underpins the notion of a long-term 'movement'. The crusades, then, were not confined to the Middle Ages. The Riley-Smith definition also embraces what has been termed the 'pluralist' idea that crusades were fought not only against Muslims in the Middle East, the basis of popular understandings of the term, but also against Muslims in Spain, Cathar heretics in southern France, pagans in north-eastern Europe, and political opponents of the papacy, amongst others. The crusades to the eastern Mediterranean were accorded a special status and served as the benchmark against which other crusades were defined. But the expansion of our understanding of where crusades could happen, and against whom, means that the automatic link that people regularly make with Christian versus Muslim warfare is incorrect.

The definition simultaneously narrows our range of reference because its precision allows us to differentiate clearly between the crusades proper and many other instances of warfare to which the word 'crusade' are often loosely but inaccurately applied. There were many occasions in the Middle Ages when Christians and Muslims fought one another but which were not technically crusades. This means that the word 'crusade', if used accurately, cannot serve as the leitmotif for all Christian-Muslim interaction in the medieval period. (In any event, much of this interaction was not to do with warfare at all.) By paying careful attention to issues of definition, we are also able to see the crusades as historically discrete entities, each one specific to the time and circumstances in which it took place. This might seem an obvious point, but it is noteworthy how often one comes across a statement such as 'Richard the Lionheart came back from the crusades'. Not really: King Richard I of England, came back from one particular expedition which took place between 1188 and 1192, an expedition which since the eighteenth century has conventionally been called the 'Third Crusade'. The frequent misuse of the plural 'crusades' gives the impression of the historical crusades as a relentlessly ongoing process, and by extension as a sort of ambient mood which helped to set the tone for life in the Middle Ages generally.

It is perhaps inevitable that, despite the enormous academic interest shown in the crusades in recent decades, it is to the impressionistic and imprecise images of crusading that people revert when the issue of contemporary relevance arises. Nowhere is this more vividly illustrated than in the responses to the terrible events of 9/11. The word 'crusade' entered the public domain very soon after the disaster and, interestingly, from more than one direction. President George W. Bush himself was quick to use the term to describe his war on terrorism. This piece of rhetoric had to be swiftly abandoned because it became clear that it was offensive to the leaders and populations of those pro-Western Arab states that Bush needed to court if his campaign against terrorists was to be successful. But the cat was out of the bag, and the notion that there is some sort of connection between the war on terrorism and the crusades has persisted.

In this, it has been reinforced by the rhetoric of Usama bin Laden and his supporters, who have tapped into a seam of Muslim hostility towards the West by referring to the Americans and their allies as 'crusaders'. This is not a new trick, but it has acquired a new force. When, during the first Gulf War in 1991, Saddam Hussein described his opponents as 'crusaders', this was met with mild bemusement in the West. If anything, it seemed to show how strangely out of touch political discourse in the Arab world could be, a prejudice reinforced by the regular use of the same crusading language by the Libyan leader Colonel Qaddafi, whom President Ronald Reagan famously dismissed as a 'Looney Toon'. But when Usama bin Laden used the word 'crusaders' to describe the West, the effect was altogether more sinister; and by virtue of its being more sinister, the perception developed that it must actually have a more momentous historical grounding than used to be appreciated.

The problem here is that all sides in the post-9/11 war of words are guilty of forcing historical continuity out of discontinuity. They are falling for what might be described as the 'wormhole effect'. A wormhole is a pseudo-scientific phenomenon beloved of science fiction writers and movie makers to get round the unhelpful tendency of the laws of physics to spoil a good story. Wormholes are the supposed entrances to mysterious galactic shortcuts that enable someone to move quickly from A to B on the other side of the universe without having to traverse the enormous distances in between. The intervening distance is effectively collapsed to nothingness, and A and B stand in relation to each other exactly as if they were physically adjacent. As with imaginary space travel, so with history at the hands of politicians, demagogues, journalists, media commentators and, it must be said, academic historians flattered by the thought that their bit of the remote past actually matters in the real world. The wormhole effect is what happens when a piece of the past, A, is brought into immediate contact with a piece of the present, B, without asking awkward questions about what happened in the interval between them.

A further problem is that the word 'crusade' tends to be used in different ways and evokes diverse, even contradictory, sets of associations. One often comes across the word used metaphorically, in contexts far removed from medieval warfare between Westerners and Muslims, to denote worthwhile causes. General Eisenhower's account of the Allied struggle against Germany in 1944–5 was entitled *Crusade in Europe*. Batman is the Caped Crusader. There are crusades against poverty, illiteracy, social injustice and crime, for example. Drug tsars wage crusades against drug barons. This metaphorical usage is much more common in English than in other European languages, a reflection of the fact that the word caught on among nineteenth-century Christian evangelical movements in various parts of the English-speaking world. To describe a movement for religious renewal as a 'crusade' was to tap into a sense of go-ahead, muscular religiosity: Christianity set to the hymn 'Onward Christian Soldiers' and lit by stained-glass windows depicting a clean-limbed St George slaying the dragon.

This evangelical appropriation of the word 'crusade' is still current, especially in the United States. It is almost certainly this usage, and not an understanding of medieval history in itself, which ultimately fed into President Bush's remarks. The religious roots of the crusade-as-metaphor have interesting implications. It is easy to see why the language of conflict can be extended to many facets of human endeavour, but it is noteworthy that 'crusade' prompts associations that other conflict-words cannot accommodate as easily: 'battle', for example, suggests something over and done with quite quickly; 'fight' is too neutral; 'struggle' admits the possibility of defeat. To say that someone is waging a crusade, however, is to register something very positive. In the first place, it implies that the cause fought for is just and something that fair-minded people can unite behind: drug tsars crusade against drug barons, but not the other way round. Second, a crusade is something that takes dogged perseverance: modern-day crusaders are in it for the long haul and will not be deflected by short-term setbacks in their pursuit of final victory. And third, a crusade not only helps its intended beneficiaries – crime victims, junkies, the poor or whoever – but also does credit to those doing the crusading. (Interestingly, in this respect at least the metaphorical meaning of 'crusade' actually finds an echo in medieval Europeans' understanding of the real, historical crusades as legitimate, difficult-but-necessary and morally improving ventures.)

On the other hand, the historical crusades themselves tend to evoke very negative responses. The real crusades are often seen as a clear demonstration, perhaps the ultimate demonstration, of medieval Europeans' limitations. They were the perfect opportunities, it seems, to put narrow-mindedness, religious intolerance, and uncontrolled aggression into bloody practice. As with the positive evangelical metaphor, this condemnation is rooted in older judgements, in this instance the horrified disapproval of Enlightenment thinkers who regarded the crusades as the argument-clinching proof of the depths to which unrestrained, superstitious, priest-infested societies were capable of sinking. This Enlightenment disdain has been hardened in more recent times by the bitter lessons of history: the Holocaust in particular has shown how appalling the consequences of racial-religious hatreds can be. Post-colonial sensitivities have also been a factor. In the nineteenth and early twentieth centuries historians studying the crusades were often gung-ho about making connections between the medieval and contemporary European expansion. This was especially the case in France, which developed colonial interests in parts of the Arab-speaking world. After the Second World War and the collapse of the European empires, colonization became a source of embarrassment, and because the crusades had been seen as proto-colonial trial runs for the spread of Western civilization, their reputation duly suffered by association.

The strength of feeling that the crusades can arouse is remarkable. In 2000, for example, no less a figure than Pope John Paul II felt moved to express regret for the harm that Christians in the past had done to others in the name of religion. In 2004 he apologized for the sack of Constantinople by the army of the Fourth Crusade in 1204. 1204 was a busy year: 2004 was also the eight-hundredth anniversary of the conquest of Normandy by the armies of the king of France. Normandy had been ruled by the kings of England for most of the previous 138 years, ever since Duke William II of Normandy seized the English throne in 1066. But not a whisper of apology from the French government in 2004. Apologizing for something that took place eight centuries before would be downright laughable. Yet mention the crusades and somehow all this common sense gets lost in a fit of well-intentioned but grossly misinformed hand-wringing.

Interestingly, the negative image of the crusades has also been fed by an uncritically rosy and simplistic image of the medieval Islamic world. The origins of this image are complex: Western post-colonial contrition, political correctness, ignorance, inverted Orientalism and cultural relativism all contribute to the mix. But the main impetus is the need to construct an 'Other' off which to bounce the sorts of stereotypes about the medieval West that we considered in Chapter 1. Intolerant, barbaric zealots fighting other intolerant, barbaric zealots is one thing; intolerant, barbaric zealots fighting sophisticated, civilized people rather like ourselves is quite another, and something to savour if one's taste is for Morality Lite. One often reads in non-academic contexts, for example, that while western Europe was struggling out of the Dark Ages, the Muslim world was far more advanced, with schools and libraries, systems of public sanitation, sophisticated agricultural techniques, an openness to scientific enquiry and intellectual curiosity, and a culture of religious tolerance. Now, the point with this image, as with many such stereotypes, is that it does indeed have some basis in fact, in large part because when Islam exploded out of its Arabian heartland in the seventh and eighth centuries, it absorbed and adapted many of the

elements that it encountered in the late Roman and Persian civilizations at whose expense it grew. If one had to identify the place in
Europe in the year 1000 with the most sophisticated culture, the place
to choose would not be the courts of the kings of England, France or
Germany, not Rome, and probably not even Constantinople, the capital of the Byzantine successors to the Roman Empire, but Córdoba,
Seville and the other urban centres of the Muslim Ummayad caliphate
in Spain.

On the other hand, stereotypes work by oversimplifying an image
and then freezing it across time and space. To speak of 'medieval Islam'
is in fact to consider a wide range of social, cultural, economic and
political forms. At different times and in different places one encounters urbanized communities and traditional tribal groupings; intellectual openness and rigid defence of tradition; studied religious tolerance
and holy-war fervour. More to the point, these and other oppositions
were often present simultaneously in given parts of the Muslim world,
with the result that Muslim polities were dynamic, shifting quantities,
not the settings for fixed-in-stone verities. A good illustration of the
potential for internal variety comes from Spain. Soon after 1000 the
Ummayad caliphate in fact proved to be politically fragile, and it splin-
tered into numerous petty statelets known as the 'taifas'. This frag-
mentation increased the relative strength of the Christian polities of
northern Spain, hitherto overshadowed by their Muslim neighbours to
the south. They began to exert pressure on the Muslims, first by means
of demands for tribute payments and then, gradually, through territo-
rial expansion. In 1085 the Christian king of Leon-Castile, Alfonso VI,
took control of the city of Toledo in the middle of the Iberian peninsula. This represented a significant southward shift in the boundary
between the areas of Muslim and Christian control, and it caused great
alarm among the Spanish Muslim leaders.

Their response was to invite in the military assistance of the
Almoravids, a coalition of north-west African tribes that had grown up
through a combination of military expansionism and appeals to religious purity – what might loosely be termed 'fundamentalism', as long
as we remember that this word was only coined in the nineteenth century. The appeal for help worked all too well: the Almoravids soon
pushed Alfonso back onto the defensive and in due course took over
control of most of Muslim Spain for themselves. One of the leading
taifa rulers, Al-Mu'tamid of Seville, when pondering the merits of invit-
ing the Almoravids across the Straits of Gibraltar, is reported to have
said that he would prefer to pasture camels than to herd pigs. What

might look like a throwaway remark in fact contains a great deal of compressed meaning: the reference to pigs evokes the fact that the eating of pork is forbidden to Muslims but not Christians, and the camels conjure up a picture of the Almoravids as a primitive society that had not progressed from it sub-Saharan roots, in contradistinction to the urban civilization and culture of Muslim Spain. In the end, Al-Mu'tamid opted for the unpalatable coreligionists rather than the unpalatable infidels. But the fact that this sort of doubt could be expressed at all is a reminder that we must not create a caricature of medieval Islam as a homogenous bloc: precisely the mistake, that is, made by modern advocates of the 'relevant' crusades.

It is not difficult to see how, since 9/11, the crusades have become sucked more than ever into debates about the origins of current problems. One of the most notable effects of 9/11 was that it generated a real public appetite for historical understanding. This was most evident in the United States, of course, but was also to be found in other Western countries. Before 9/11 there was a sense that history was not quite what it used to be. The most fashionable history book in recent years had been Francis Fukuyama's *The End of History and the Last Man* (1992), which argued that, with the end of the Cold War, there would be no further ideological conflicts to drive historical change, and the world would settle down to enjoy the benefits of a largely uncontested system of liberal democratic capitalism. It was a very complacent message. But Fukuyama's creed resonated with people living in historically unparalleled levels of comfort and security in the West. Tellingly, among popular histories around this time there was a large market for books on the Second World War, as exemplified by *The Greatest Generation* (1999) by the NBC newscaster Tom Brokaw. These books fed the wistful notion that the generation that had lived through the War, people for so long a central presence in our lives but now sadly passing from the scene, had participated in *real* history. They had been part of an epic story that had given them a sense of nobility and purpose, something that later generations could not replicate. Nothing that big seemed to happen any more. And then, at 8.43 Eastern Time on 11 September 2001, American Airlines Flight 11 from Boston to Los Angeles smashed into the north tower of the World Trade Center, and history started all over again.

The sense that something historically momentous had happened took hold very quickly, even as people were reeling from the initial shock and grief. To begin with, the historical impulse went off in the opposite direction: that is to say, the question that the US broadcast and print media ran with most insistently was how the events of 9/11 would be seen in future historical perspective. If recourse was made to the past, it tended to focus on the (not very compelling) parallels with the Japanese attack on Pearl Harbor in December 1941. Only more gradually did people start to ask questions with a real historical dimension. What had motivated the suicide hijackers? What made Usama bin Laden an influential figure among many anti-Western Muslims? Was the avowed religious fanaticism of Al-Qaeda its genuine impetus, or a cover for other agendas? In addition to thinking about obvious and immediate explanations, such as the running problem of Muslim hostility towards American-backed Israel, vexed Western relations with various Arab regimes, and the widespread perception in the Arab world that it was being left behind in the growth of global prosperity, consideration was also given to the supposed existence of a more deep-rooted, almost transcendental, clash of civilizations and value systems, a continuation of a centuries-long struggle that had been identified by the eighteenth-century historian Edward Gibbon when he wrote of the 'world's debate' and was latterly, and more prosaically, evoked by titles such as Benjamin Barber's *Jihad vs. McWorld* (1995) and Samuel Huntington's *The Clash of Civilizations?* (1992).

The problem here is the reliance on continuities that have no historical basis. From the Western side of things, modern research has, as we have seen, been pushing the chronological boundaries of the crusading movement beyond its traditional 1291 terminus and into the early modern era. But this does not mean that there has not been a clear break with the past since then; the crusades did not live on indefinitely. The most important shift took place in the eighteenth and nineteenth centuries, when the holy-war ideology that had underpinned crusading fell out of favour. Crusading had been built on the belief that violence in itself is a morally neutral quantity: it is the status of those authorizing the violence, the state of mind of the people doing the violence, and the reasons why they are doing it, which govern its moral value. Since the Enlightenment, however, the idea has developed that violence is intrinsically morally negative: it can be used in certain limited situations, but only as a necessary evil. Once this shift in perceptions took hold, there was a decisive break with the crusading past. Significantly, when people enthused about the crusades in the nineteenth century, they tended to do so by assimilating them into the story of chivalry, which as we saw in Chapter 1 was one of the elements of medieval culture that nineteenth-century observers found most congenial, not with reference to an increasingly alien-seeming body of holy-war thought.

Much is sometimes made of the utterances of recent historical actors to suggest that a sense of continuity did indeed survive. In 1917, for example, when General Allenby led his British troops into Jerusalem during a campaign against the Ottoman Turks, he is supposed to have remarked 'Today the wars of the crusaders are completed'.[17] Similarly when in 1920 the French general Henri Gouraud entered Damascus to become the military governor of Syria, he is believed to have said 'Behold, Saladin, we have returned!'[18] But these were only attempts by non-historians to capture something of their sense of importance, not considered historical judgements (and in both cases the quotations may be apocryphal anyway). The crusades are much more remote from our experience that we sometimes imagine. When nineteenth-century politicians wrestled with the 'Eastern Question', they were not reviving crusading thought but pondering the secular, geopolitical implications of the decline of the Ottoman Empire. And the growth of the metaphorical use of the word 'crusade' that we have seen in the nineteenth and twentieth centuries was only made possible by a corresponding ideological and cultural distancing from the thought world of the literal, historical crusades.

The same picture of discontinuity emerges on the Muslim side. In the Ottoman period memories of the crusades lingered among some intellectuals and in folktales, but not in any systematic way. The notion of Islamic holy war, *jihad*, lost much of its topicality and emotional force in the sixteenth and seventeenth centuries. It was only around the middle of the nineteenth century that Muslims writers and thinkers began to revive awareness of the history of the crusades as a response to Western imperialist expansion: the Muslims had 'won' the crusades, the theory went, so they were a comforting and inspiring symbol of what renewed resistance could achieve. Interestingly, the modern Arabic term for the crusades – *Hurub al-Salibiyya*, 'the wars of the cross' – dates from that time as a translation of the terminology encountered in Western history books. It is not a medieval survival. It was probably only towards the middle of the twentieth century that the crusades entered the broad public consciousness in the Arab world, and then in the Muslim world more generally. The critical moment here was the creation in 1948 of the state of Israel. Israel's borders, in particular since 1967, approximate to those of the twelfth-century Latin Kingdom of Jerusalem, the most important of the Latin polities created in Palestine and Syria in the wake of the First Crusade. This apparent correspondence has helped to foster the idea of the present as a cyclical revisiting of the past. The fact that Israel is a Jewish state, whereas the Latin Kingdom was ruled by Christians, is not a problem: in modern anti-Western rhetoric, the 'Zionists' and Western 'crusaders' are seen as two prongs of a single assault on Islam.

Although fundamentalists couch the opposition between Islam and the West in religious terms, and this consequently lends a particular edge to the evocation of crusading as a manifestation of Western aggression, it is noteworthy that the crusades have also been mobilized in ways which speak to wider issues of political and economic empowerment in the face of Western hegemony around the world. For example, in Egypt in the early 1960s, the regime of Colonel Nasser, whose ideology was grounded in Arab nationalism rather than in Islamicism, diverted large amounts of money into the production of a movie called *Saladin the Triumphant*. This was made on an epic scale and, unusually for that time and place, in colour. Saladin was the twelfth-century warlord who led the Muslim attacks against the Latin Christian states in Syria and Palestine, an offensive which culminated in 1187 with a crushing defeat of the Latin armies and the capture of Jerusalem, which had been in Christian hands since it fell to the forces of the First Crusade in 1099. Saladin also unified Syria and Egypt, which was one of Nasser's cherished political aims. The film, starring Ahmed Mazhar who was at that time the most famous leading man in Arab cinema, came out in 1963. Clearly, when audiences were presented with vivid images of Saladin overcoming the Franks, they were being invited to make a connection with their contemporary experience, in particular the Suez Crisis of 1956. In that year British and French forces, with diversionary support from Israel, had invaded Egypt to retake control of the Suez Canal, which Nasser's regime had nationalized. The Israeli forces acquitted themselves well, but the Anglo-French operation, despite military successes on the ground, proved a political fiasco. Nasser was therefore able to present the affair as a victory of Arab arms over the Western invader. As Nasser and his filmmakers could see, Saladin was a potent symbol for Arab defiance and of faith in ultimate victory.

On both sides of the 'world's debate', therefore, we find the crusades resurrected in order to invest modern political, religious and cultural agendas with a feeling of historical gravitas. They help to feed the sense of being part of something momentous which has been building up in some parts of the Muslim world since the mid-twentieth century, and which was reawakened in the West by 9/11. As long as people *believe* that there is a real historical connection, and many people clearly do, then it might be argued that the connection is indeed legitimate, because what matter are the stories and images that people take from their imagined past in order to construct their identities, not the technical details of historical 'truth'. Yes, up to a point; but the current misappropriation of the crusades is so rampant that it has become necessary to stand by the distinction between what actually happened in the past and what some people would like to have happened. The two things *are* different.

In any event, the true relevance of the crusades is nothing to do with how they may or may not help to explain the modern world. It is about the mental adjustments that we must make if we want to understand the crusaders and their world without importing anachronistic value judgements. Perhaps one of the biggest challenges faced by anyone studying the Middle Ages is to unthink a raft of modern assumptions and values about the morality of violence, because only then is it possible to understand how people with entirely different approaches were able to function. In this respect, the crusades are simply one vivid and topical illustration of where the relevance of medieval history truly lies. The crusades demonstrate the complete 'alterity' of the Middle Ages: that is to say, the notion that when we mentally project ourselves into the medieval past, what we will find is an alien environment in which the differences from our own experience impress themselves upon us far more than the similarities, which are likely to be superficial anyway. The term 'alterity', like many pieces of fashionable scholarly jargon, has a whiff of look-at-me cleverness about it. It is in fact a good example of the use of different registers in English that we encountered earlier: the word's root is *alter*, the Latin for 'other', and the compound *alter-ity* directly corresponds to *other-ness*. But it is worth hanging on to the term because it gives the underlying concept a technical quality, whereas to express matters simply in terms of 'otherness' or 'difference' trivializes what is involved.

What, then, is the alterity of the Middle Ages? The first point to stress is that we are really dealing with multiple alterities. As we saw in Chapter 2, there is no single and quintessential state of medieval-ness to be detected in a given place or time. Alterity thus stands for a superabundance of diverse social, political, economic and cultural forms. Nor is it the case that the nature of the difference corresponds directly to the length of time that has elapsed. It would be preposterous to argue that people alive 500 years ago were three times 'more like us' than people living 1500 years ago.

So where is all this difference? The most obvious area, and the one most susceptible to modern stereotyping in visual media such as films and games, is the material environment in which people lived: their physical appearance, their diet, their clothing, their technologies, their habitats. Clearly, for anyone travelling back in time to the Middle Ages, these sorts of differences would dominate their first impressions (though not, one suspects, the enduring ones). It is easy to think of a host of ways in which our lives are fundamentally different. Turn on the ignition in your car, take an aspirin, pick up the phone: countless routine operations nowadays place us in a very unmedieval world. But in itself this observation is too obvious to form the basis of a justification for studying the Middle Ages. One does not need to know any medieval history to be aware that the automotive, pharmaceutical and telecommunications industries, to use just our three examples, are post-medieval phenomena. All times and places are historically specific and therefore discrete and unique. The surprising thing would be if people in the Middle Ages *did* live like us!

This is not to trivialize the importance of analyzing the external, physical domain when forming judgements about societies in the past. It is simply that this in itself is an inadequate basis for an understanding of alterity. The crucial thing is to look beyond the material manifestations of a historical subject, and into the mental spaces that people occupied. Broadly speaking, this extra dimension is what distinguishes academic history from antiquarian enthusiasm, which tends to focus exclusively on the physical differences between the past and present. The exploration of the past's mental worlds, it should be noted, applies just as much to those scholarly disciplines such as art history and archaeology which deal directly with the physical remains of the past, as it does to other subjects, such as history and literature, in which the study of surviving artefacts is just one part of a wider methodological repertoire. All these subjects are ultimately concerned with the ways in which people in the past understood their world.

Ask yourself who you are, and you will very quickly get beyond the externals to some more penetrating questions about the concepts that underpin your sense of identity. Not 'Do I own a car?' but 'How does the mobility that having a car makes possible affect my mental mapping of the world around me?' Not 'Do I own a phone?' but 'How does my ability to communicate with different people influence my sense of the communities to which I belong?' On a day-to-day basis we seldom have to confront the elements that make up our sense of personhood, at least not consciously. But it is an interesting exercise to ask the questions which expose our cognitive assumptions, that is to say the basic conceptual frameworks that we carry around with us all the time in order to make sense of the world as we are bombarded with its sights and sounds. What, for example, do I think about the space around me, and how far do I attach different values to different parts of my physical world? Similarly with time. How do I map out and measure the passage of time? What stories set in or about the past resonate particularly clearly with my sense of who I am? Similarly, too, with human physicality and social interaction. What do I think about my body? What do I think about sex, and what do I think it is about men and women that makes them different? What do I think about childhood, ageing and death? Are there people whom I dislike to the extent that I define who I am in opposition to them? How do I understand the difference between 'public' and 'private', and are their formal situations and rituals in which my sense of identity is brought to the fore? Above all, how do the vocabulary and patterns of thinking that I have at my disposal to describe my world channel my thoughts in certain directions? The list of such issues could be much longer. The point is that these are fundamental questions, the answers to which will tell you much more about someone than even a minutely detailed description of his or her physical appearance and actions. And what is true of an individual is also true of societies in the past.

Historical enquiry based on these sorts of questions has become known as 'cultural history'. In this context 'culture' is understood in a totalizing sense to embrace all the ways in which people perceive the world and function in it, rather than a narrower meaning of artistic activity. The reasons why cultural history has become fashionable since the 1960s and 70s are complex. In very broad terms, it is one manifestation of scholarly dissatisfaction with old-fashioned political history starring great men. More specifically, one of the most important influences has been the interest among French historians in the study of *mentalités*, the conceptual grids that people use in order to function as social, economic and political beings. Significantly, many of the leading pioneers of the study of *mentalités*, such as Georges Duby, Jacques Le Goff and Jean-Claude Schmitt, have been medievalists. Medieval historians, as well as early modernists, have found cultural history so fruitful because it opens up new ways of reading source materials that can otherwise seem so sketchy, alien and opaque. A metaphor often used is that of archaeology: by drawing on the methodologies of a range of disciplines such as literary criticism and anthropology, historians can 'excavate' meanings which would otherwise lie concealed under the surface of the evidence. It is true that when one encounters some of the more abstruse or dense examples of cultural history, particularly when they are drawing on terminology borrowed from literary studies, one can find oneself pining for honest-to-goodness, empiricist history all about real people *doing things*. And, as with any fashionable approach, there are times when it can look like common sense over-packaged in scholarly jargon. Overall, however, the benefits of the growth of cultural history for our historical understanding have been enormous.

One excellent example of the rich potential of this approach is Jean-Claude Schmitt's *The Holy Greyhound* (1979; English translation 1983). The book is based on a shortish passage in the writings of a thirteenth-century Dominican inquisitor named Stephen of Bourbon. In it, Stephen describes a strange experience that he had in the remote region of the Dombes, in what is now eastern France, after he heard an intriguing story from the locals. According to this tale, which in fact has correspondences with stories told in many different cultures, a faithful dog was standing guard over his master's baby. When a snake appeared intent on killing the child, the dog successfully fought it off. The master then returned to the scene and killed the dog in the mistaken belief that it had harmed the baby. On realizing his mistake, he and his wife threw the dog's body down a well. In time, the master's home, a castle, crumbled and was forgotten, and the area was reclaimed by the forest, but the local peasants preserved the memory of the faithful dog, looked on it as a martyr, and prayed to it when they needed help. In particular, according to Stephen, women whose small children were ill would seek the advice of a local old woman, who would lead them to the site of the grave. There they would make offerings and perform certain rituals, before leaving the sick baby on its own, in the belief that the ailing child was in fact an imposter, and the real child, who had earlier been kidnapped by fauns in the woods, would be returned before the adults returned to the spot. Stephen concludes his story by describing how he took action against this practice, gathering the local people to hear a sermon denouncing their superstition, digging up the dog's remains, and burning them along with the surrounding area of supposedly sacred woodland. Anyone reviving the cult of the dog in future would, Stephen arranged with the local lord, have his possessions forfeited and sold.

On the face of it, this is a story that appears to support two well-worn caricatures of medieval society: the image of an aggressive, inflexible Church bringing its apparatus of social control and oppression down on ordinary people who just wanted to get on with their lives; and the image of medieval peasants as superstitious, uncritical primitives who were helpless in the face of dangers that they could not understand. In fact, in Schmitt's careful analysis a far more nuanced and intriguing picture emerges. Stephen of Bourbon was not at all like a journalist reporting a story observationally and locating it straightforwardly in the present. A close analysis of his text, as well as of what we can assume about his background, reveals that Stephen's reactions to the cult of the dog ('St Guinefort', as it was known) were the product of ways of seeing and thinking conditioned by his membership of a religious order, his role as an inquisitor, and his status as part of a small, mobile, powerful, highly educated intellectual elite. More than this, Stephen's perceptions are shown to be expressions of language and ways of ordering ideas that were preserved in authoritative texts, many of them written hundreds of years earlier. He was like a literary tradition in motion.

Stephen, however, belonged to the class of medieval people about whom we tend to know most because they dominate the written record. So the more exciting and ground-breaking part of Schmitt's book is his analysis of the peasants and their mental worlds. By examining a wide range of sources with a large chronological span, and by exploiting diverse scholarly approaches, including close textual analysis, anthropology, art history, folklore studies, post-medieval religious history, and archaeology, Schmitt was able to build up a rich and layered picture of the peasants' world. This included their ideas about the different sorts of spaces in their environment; their attitudes towards their aristocratic lords and masters; the values they attached to ritual; the many and subtle interactions between popular and learned culture; the peasants' understandings of the supernatural world; their reactions to illness; and their ideas about motherhood and childhood. What emerges in particular is an elucidation of the historically specific trends and influences that manifested themselves in the cult that Stephen of Bourbon encountered.

This is significant because it is sometimes the reaction, when presented with exceptional evidence for medieval popular practice such as that found in Stephen's account, to suppose that it must be lifting the lid on timeless, ancient practices: so ancient, indeed, that they preserve the traces of pre-Christian, pagan beliefs (even though, in this particular case, an area like the Dombes had been formally Christian for many centuries). In fact, even when Schmitt ranges very widely for clues (he notes, for example, analogues between St Guinefort's cult and folk-medicine practised in parts of France as late as the twentieth century), he is drawing out the historical distinctiveness of the situation that Stephen found. If anything, it is Stephen, with his mindset largely conditioned by centuries-old texts, who comes across as the 'traditional' character, whereas the peasants emerge as adaptable and creative figures playing out a unique synthesis between, on the one hand, cultural and religious influences that had only recently entered their world, and, on the other, more venerable patterns of thinking and behaving. This is not, then, a study in timeless peasant-ness, but an exploration of a distinctive, and very different, world.

The case of St Guinefort is one celebrated example of the importance of alterity as the key to why the Middle Ages are relevant to us. Medieval people were different, not only from ourselves but also from each other. In an age when many people are uneasy about the flattening out of cultural differences around the world because of globalization, and when we are being increasingly told that we are simply the visible manifestations of characteristics locked deterministically into our DNA, it is vitally important to understand the liberating richness of human diversity, across time as well as space. To this end, the Middle Ages are indisputably relevant.

Conclusion

One of the most enduring and quaint stereotypes about life in the Middle Ages relates to how we imagine people back then spoke. For what people spoke in the Middle Ages, of course, was 'Mock Medieval'. It crops up time and again in films and popular literature. Excruciatingly, English Heritage, one of the main organizations responsible for historical sites in England, pays actors to dress in period costume and improvise dialogue in Mock Medieval for the benefit, if that is the word, of bemused and embarrassed tourists. The effect is very familiar: 'Yonder lies the castle of my father' Tony Curtis famously remarks in *The Black Shield of Falworth* (1954), not 'That's my father's castle over there'. Mock Medieval is a gift to satirists, and it is so inescapably self-parodic that it is amazing that authors and script writers persist with it. But they do. The medieval characters in *Timeline*, for instance, talk the medieval talk, at least in the early stages of the book before Crichton tires of it. Mock Medieval even seeps its way into the dialogue of films which self-consciously parade their use of modern idiom. 'What say you, friar?' Kevin Costner asks in *Robin Hood: Prince of Thieves* (1991). Mock Medieval overlaps with another filmic and pop-cultural convention, the American caricature of over-enunciated and over-elaborate British speech. In fact, Mock Medieval tends to sound most convincing delivered in a British accent (which is very good news for members of British Equity). No matter that, in fact, British Received Pronunciation ('posh' BBC English) is a wholly post-medieval accent, whereas some American accents are probably as close as we will ever get nowadays to how English was spoken around 1600 and so, at a push, what it might have sounded like at the end of the Middle Ages!

Mock Medieval in modern-day culture is a pastiche of what started out as a serious-minded attempt in the eighteenth and nineteenth centuries to convey the ways in which it was believed medieval people did talk to one another. Walter Scott, for instance, made a point of distancing himself from those earlier writers who had peppered their medieval characters' dialogue with recherché and archaic terms to the point that they became incomprehensible. Keep the vocabulary basically contemporary, Scott argued, but use the speech rhythms and grammatical features of bygone days to convey the characters' medieval quality. For example, towards the end of *Ivanhoe*, King Richard declares to the slippery Grand Master of the Templars:

> Be it so...but for thine own sake tax me not with usurpation now. – Dissolve thy Chapter, and depart with thy followers to thy next Preceptory, (if thou canst find one) which has not been made the scene of treasonable conspiracy against the King of England – Or, if thou wilt, remain, to share our hospitality, and to behold our justice.[19]

Part of Scott's skill was making people sound simultaneously different and comprehensible, and the same balancing act remains the basis for Mock Medieval. Mock Medieval pastiches the language of Shakespeare and the Authorized Version (King James) Bible, with all its sonority and gravitas. In fact this is about as far back as it is practical to go in the quest for anything remotely resembling Mock. Any further back than the English of Shakespeare's day, in other words to *actual* medieval English, and the grammar, vocabulary and spelling start to put up more and more barriers to easy understanding. The equivalents of English Mock Medieval in other European languages are similarly based on the same sorts of highly selective borrowings and anachronistic fudges.

For our purposes, the interest of Mock Medieval goes beyond its being yet another funny example of the liberties that people take with the Middle Ages. For what lies under the surface of Mock, the thing that makes it sound all right even though only a moment's reflection exposes its ludicrous conceit, is an unspoken sense that medieval people were odd and they knew it. Mock has the effect of casting medieval men and women as the dimly self-aware spokespersons of a sense of difference and detachment that in reality, of course, only exists in our modern perception of them, not in their own contemporary awareness. They probably could not quite put their finger on it, so Mock implies, but they somehow sensed that they were primitive, undeveloped, crude, or whatever stereotype one wants to apply, and that better times, progress, lay somewhere in the future. Mock, in other words, makes medieval people sound like actors in their own costume drama: hence English

Heritage's pandering to the idea that if you have people dressed up in old-looking clothes, it sounds wrong if they speak in an unaffected modern idiom. But that is, of course, preposterous. If two people were having a relaxed, informal conversation in, say, Old High German or Old French, translating this into modern idiom will capture the flavour of what they were saying much better than will Mock. In a way, Mock dehumanizes; it turns real people into cardboard cut-outs. Seen in these terms, the dislocating effect of Mock looks silly, of course. But its tenacious survival in popular culture is a useful reminder of how easy it is to dragoon medieval people into a world which is wholly of our making, not theirs, and to force on them ways of thinking and behaving that would not have been current at the time.

In addition to populating medieval society with funny-sounding caricatures, popular culture seizes on the Middle Ages to satisfy its craving for pattern and meaning in the past. There is an enormous market for conspiracy-theory history about cover-ups, secret organizations, codes hidden in pictures, the truth that 'they' have tried to suppress, persecutions, lost civilizations and the whole bric-a-brac of brainless pseudo-history. Not all of this is medieval, of course: think about how much mileage there has been for writers and publishers in the lost city of Atlantis or in the Pyramids. But the Middle Ages are the setting for more than their fair share of this nonsense, and they have contributed a rich line-up of characters and motifs to the mix: the Merovingian kings of Francia, the Cathar heretics, the Templars, King Arthur, the Round Table, the Holy Grail, secret scrolls, hidden treasure, the discovery of America before Columbus, the Turin Shroud, the Inquisition, monks, the Church in general. In casting the medieval Church as a villain in many of it stories, incidentally, a lot of this stuff, by British writers at any rate, reads strangely like a continuation by other means of the sort of anti-Catholic rhetoric that was current between the sixteenth and nineteenth centuries. This is just one demonstration of how bizarrely misconceived and old-fashioned these books can appear even before one begins to unpick the silliness of their conspiracy theories. Perhaps the landmark publication which kicked off this vogue (though it had antecedents in fantasist literature) was Henry Lincoln, Richard Leigh and Michael Baigent's *Holy Blood, Holy Grail* (1982). Many imitations have appeared since then.

It might be objected that attacking this sort of garbage is picking on a soft target. Fair enough. But the point is that the fantasists do not inhabit their own private world. Their works construct themselves rhetorically in opposition to mainstream academic history while simultaneously mimicking many of its methodologies, and there are various hybrid forms which deliberately blur the distinction between legitimate and bogus historiography. Consider, for example, the remarks of Sean Martin in his best-selling *The Knights Templar: The History and Myths of the Legendary Military Order* (2004). The Templars were an order of knight-monks formed in the twelfth century and famously suppressed in 1307–12. They therefore obeyed the first rule of conspiracy-theory history, which is to create a mystique around oneself by coming to a sudden and sticky end. In this the Templars form a stark contrast to the other main Military Order, the Hospitallers, who plodded on for centuries after 1312 and eventually mutated into modern-day organizations as mysterious and sinister as the St John's Ambulance Brigade. Martin's book is for the most part a fairly straight piece of popular history, but towards the end he tries to have it both ways, playing on the ambiguities in his choice of title and appealing to the market for what he calls 'speculative', in opposition to 'orthodox', history. Evoking Umberto Eco, whose *Foucault's Pendulum* (1988) is a brilliant attack on conspiracy-theory history, he writes:

> Umberto Eco points out that the conspiracy theorists tend to project a great deal of their own failings into their theories, no matter how wild. What he does not examine, however, is that the hands that write the more standard, orthodox history can also be driven by similar forces: the desire for peer acceptance; the desire to maintain one's position within academe; and, perhaps, more importantly, one's funding, all of which would be severely compromised by entertaining the more mythical version of the Templar story. The latter [i.e. orthodox] approach ignores anything vaguely speculative about the Order, and, in doing so, perpetuates a blinkered and restricted view of history.[20]

Well, no. There is just intellectually honest history and intellectually dishonest history, and all the relativism in the world cannot wish this basic distinction away. For the real point about pseudo-history is not that it appeals to a caste of mind that likes its heroes alive and well in caves, waiting in suspended animation for the very right occasion to come along. It is about easy answers. Easy answers made to look complicated by being decked out in lost parchments, secret signs, hidden codes and all the other gimmicks, but in essence visions of how long stretches of human history boil down to simple stories, which, once unearthed despite 'their' best efforts to keep us from the truth, make everything fall beautifully into place.

In a way, therefore, the sort of rubbishy medieval history peddled by pseudo-historians is one manifestation of popular culture's insistence on simplifying the Middle Ages as far as possible. For by reducing medieval civilization to some sort of imagined essence, the stereotypes and misconceptions that we encountered in Chapter 1 are not only made possible but also lent legitimacy. Popular culture simply cannot cope with diversity, complexity, the exceptions to rules, the absence of rules. As we have seen, there are various images and associations available to us when we think medieval. Some are frivolous and fun: no expert on medieval fortresses will be unduly threatened by the sight of the castle in the Disney Magic Kingdom. Some are the stuff of self-conscious cultural reference, as in Marsellus getting medieval on Zed's ass. Some are the residue of political and cultural debates that have long since lost their topicality. But some have a real and dark resonance. To use the word 'medieval' in the trial of an alleged war-criminal, or to bandy the crusades around in reflections on the mass-murder of 9/11, is to make some very powerful points about the Middle Ages. Any serious student of the period must engage with this fact.

It all comes down to alterity. For alterity does not exist in the singular: it does not reduce to how different 'they' all were from all of 'us'. Alterity is about the tremendous variety within and between medieval cultures. If, despite the allure of pop-cultural over-simplifications, despite the bludgeoning effect of unwieldy and unhelpful historical labels, despite the inadequacies and difficulties of the evidence, despite the distraction of demands for facile relevance, we still manage to find that medieval people were fascinatingly diverse, then the same must, thank goodness, be true of us as well.

Notes

1 Michael Crichton, *Timeline* (Arrow Books: London, 2000), p. 196.
2 BBC News 12 February 2002: 'Transcript: Carla Del Ponte's address': <http://news.bbc.co.uk/1/hi/world/europe/1816719.stm>
3 Anthony Browne, 'Racism, rude names and the children of McCarthy', *The Times*, 13 February 2003.
4 Magnus Linklater, 'Those whom the gods wish to destroy, they first make famous (and then mad)', *The Times*, 6 February 2003.
5 John Carr, 'Schismatic monks hoist barricades', *The Times*, 28 January 2003.
6 Horace Walpole, *The Castle of Otranto*, ed. M. Gamer (London, 2001), p. 6.
7 Edmund Burke, *Reflections on the Revolution in France*, ed. J. C. D. Clark (Stanford, 2001), p. 238.
8 Gustave Flaubert, *Madame Bovary*, trans. G. Wall with a preface by M. Roberts (London, 2003), p. 35.
9 I. Anstruther, *The Knight and the Umbrella: An Account of the Eglinton Tournament 1839* (London, 1963), pp. 173–5.
10 Mark Twain, *Life on the Mississippi*, ed. H. Beaver (London, 1962), pp. 270–1.
11 *Ibid.*, pp. 303–4.
12 *Night and Day*, 9 September 1937, in Graham Greene, *The Pleasure-Dome: The Collected Film Criticism 1935–40*, ed. J. Russell Taylor (London, 1972), p. 166.
13 E. Le Roy Ladurie, *Montaillou: Cathars and Catholics in a French Village, 1294–1324*, trans. B. Bray (London, 1978), p. 356.
14 P. Baty, 'Clarke lays into useless history', *Times Higher Educational Supplement*, 9 May 2003.
15 Victor Hugo, *Notre-Dame de Paris 1482*, ed. G. Chamarat and G. Gengembre (Paris, 1998), appendix p. xxxvi.
16 Bede, *The Ecclesiastical History of the English People*, ed. J. McClure and R. Collins (Oxford, 1994), p. 27.
17 E. Siberry, *The New Crusaders: Images of the Crusades in the Nineteenth and Early Twentieth Centuries* (Aldershot, 2000), p. 95.
18 A. Knobler, 'Saint Louis and French Political Culture', in L. J. Workman and K. Verduin (eds), *Medievalism in Europe II* (Studies in Medievalism 8; Woodbridge, 1997), p. 168.
19 *Ivanhoe*, ed. G. Tulloch (London, 2000), p. 393.
20 S. Martin, *The Knights Templar: The History and Myths of the Legendary Military Order* (Harpenden, 2004), pp. 143–4.

Suggested Reading

Chapter 1   Popular Images of the Middle Ages

For some thoughtful comments on the relationship between academic medieval history and popular culture, see W. C. Jordan, 'Saving Medieval History; or, the New Crusade', in J. Van Engen (ed.), *The Past and Future of Medieval Studies* (Notre Dame, 1994), pp. 259–72. For the Middle Ages in the movies, see S. Airlie, 'Strange Eventful Histories: The Middle Ages in the Cinema', in P. Linehan and J. L. Nelson (eds), *The Medieval World* (London, 2001), pp. 163–83. A stimulating overview of the current state of medieval history is found in J. M. H. Smith, 'Introduction: Regarding Medievalists: Contexts and Approaches', in M. Bentley (ed.), *Companion to Historiography* (London, 1997), pp. 105–16. See also the perceptive comments of L. Patterson, 'On the Margin: Postmodernism, Ironic History, and Medieval Studies', *Speculum*, 65 (1990), pp. 87–108. N. F. Cantor, *Inventing the Middle Ages: The Lives, Works, and Ideas of the Great Medievalists of the Twentieth Century* (New York, 1991) is an entertaining, if partial and sometimes tendentious, account of the growth of the discipline. For a very engaging analysis of the issues facing ancient historians, which has many lessons for medievalists, see N. Morley, *Writing Ancient History* (London, 1999). For some important medievalist contributions to debates about the nature of history and historiography, see G. M. Spiegel, *The Past as Text: The Theory and Practice of Medieval Historiography* (Baltimore, 1997) and N. Partner, *Writing Medieval History* (London, 2005).

The ways in which the past is packaged and consumed in modern culture are divertingly explored in two books by David Lowenthal: *The Past is a Foreign Country* (Cambridge, 1985), and *The Heritage Crusade and the Spoils of History* (Cambridge, 1998). Also of interest is S. Watson, 'Touring the Medieval: Tourism, Heritage and Medievalism in Northumbria', in T. Shippey and M. Arnold (eds), *Appropriating the Medieval: Scholarship, Politics, Fraud* (Cambridge, 2001), pp. 239–61. The images associated with ancient Egypt are discussed in C. Frayling, *The Face of Tutankhamun* (London, 1992).

The script of *Pulp Fiction* has been published as Quentin Tarantino, *Pulp Fiction* (London, 1994). For a good study of the film which draws out its use of pop-cultural references, see D. Polan, *Pulp Fiction* (London, 2000). See also the celebrated, if sometimes impenetrable, essay by Carolyn Dinshaw, 'Getting Medieval: *Pulp Fiction*, Foucault, and the Uses of the Past', in her *Getting Medieval: Sexualities and Communities, Pre- and Postmodern* (Durham, NC, 1999), pp. 183–206. For the work of Michael Crichton (before *Timeline*), see E. A. Trembley, *Michael Crichton: A Critical Companion* (Westport, Conn., 1996).

Carl Bildt's frustrated reactions to the failure of his diplomatic efforts in the Balkans are expressed in his *Peace Journey: The Struggle for Peace in Bosnia* (London, 1998).

A good modern edition of Mark Twain's *A Connecticut Yankee at King Arthur's Court* is available in the Penguin Classics series, edited by J. Kaplan (Harmondsworth, 1971). This reproduces some of the illustrations by Dan Beard that appeared in the 1889 first edition. The literature on King Arthur and Arthuriana is vast. For an excellent account of the popularity of the subject, see B. Taylor and E. Brewer, *The Return of King Arthur: British and American Popular Literature since 1900* (Cambridge, 1983). There is a suggestive essay by V. M. Lagorio, 'King Arthur and Camelot, U.S.A. in the Twentieth Century', in B. Rosenthal and P. E. Szarmach (eds), *Medievalism in American Culture* (Binghamton, NY, 1989), pp. 151–69. Alfred, Lord Tennyson's *Idylls of the King* are edited by J. M. Gray, rev. edn. (London, 1996). This can be profitably read in conjunction with *Le Morte d'Arthur*, for which see *The Works of Sir Thomas Malory*, ed. E. Vinaver, rev. P. J. C. Field, 3 vols. (Oxford, 1990). For Arthur as a historical figure and his later myths, see N. J. Higham, *King Arthur: Myth-Making and History* (London, 2002).

For William Morris, see J. Banham and J. Harris (eds), *William Morris and the Middle Ages* (Manchester, 1984); and R. Furneaux Jordan, *The Medieval Vision of William Morris* (London, 1960). His *A Dream of John Ball* appears in vol. 16 of *The Collected Works of William Morris* (London, 1912; repr. 1992). For an overview of the work of the Pre-Raphaelites, see T. Hilton, *The Pre-Raphaelites* (London, 1970). For William Cobbett, see his *Rural Rides*, ed. I. Dyck (London, 2001); also A. Burton, *William Cobbett: Englishman* (London, 1997) and R. Williams, *Cobbett* (Oxford, 1983).

Horace Walpole's *The Castle of Otranto* is available in numerous editions. Among the best is that by M. Gamer for the Penguin Classics series (London, 2001), which has a good bibliography. For Walpole generally, see R. W. Ketton-Cremer, *Horace Walpole: A Biography*, 3rd edn (London, 1964), and T. Mowl, *Horace Walpole: The Great Outsider* (London, 1996). For the emergence and popularity of the Gothic novel, see the interesting account in D. Punter, *The Literature of Terror: A History of Gothic Fictions from 1765 to the Present: I: The Gothic Tradition*, 2nd edn (London, 1996). There is also a short and helpful overview of the genre in B. Hennessy, *The Gothic Novel* (London, 1978).

Medievalism has generated an extensive literature in recent decades. The ground-breaking work, which remains of great value, is A. Chandler, *A Dream of Order: The Medieval Ideal in Nineteenth-Century English Literature* (Lincoln, Nebraska, 1970; London, 1971). The series *Studies in Medievalism*, ed. L. J. Workman *et al.* is mainly pitched towards literary specialists but includes several pieces of interest to historians. See also K. L. Morris, *The Image of the Middle Ages in Romantic and Victorian Literature* (London, 1984); J. R. Dakyns. *The Middle Ages in French Literature 1851–1900* (London, 1973). For a negative appraisal of the impact of medievalism, see M. J. Wiener, *English Culture and the Decline of the Industrial Spirit, 1850–1980* (Cambridge, 1989).

For the Gothic Revival in architecture, there are useful accounts in C. Brooks, *The Gothic Revival* (London, 1999) and M. J. Lewis, *The Gothic Revival* (London,

2002). An important study of the efforts made to conserve medieval buildings is to be found in C. Dellheim, *The Face of the Past: The Preservation of the Medieval Inheritance in Victorian England* (Cambridge, 1982), which can usefully be read alongside R. Sweet, *Antiquaries: The Discovery of the Past in Eighteenth-Century Britain* (London, 2003).

Victor Hugo's *Notre-Dame de Paris* has been translated into English many times. The best recent version is by J. Sturrock (Harmondsworth, 1978). For Hugo's interest in the Middle Ages, see P. A. Ward, *The Medievalism of Victor Hugo* (University Park, PA, 1975). For Pugin and Ruskin, see A. W. N. Pugin, *Contrasts*, ed. H. R. Hitchcock, 2nd edn (Leicester, 1969) and J. Ruskin, *The Stones of Venice*, ed. J. G. Links (London, 2001). For William Beckford, see his *Vathek*, ed. R. Lonsdale (Oxford, 1998). Of interest is T. Mowl, *William Beckford, Composing for Mozart* (London, 1998).

The impact of the ideals of chivalry on nineteenth-century society has been described in a marvellous book by Mark Girouard, *The Return to Camelot: Chivalry and the English Gentleman* (London, 1981). For Chateaubriand, see B. G. Keller, *The Middle Ages Reconsidered: Attitudes in France from the Eighteenth Century through the Romantic Movement* (New York, 1994). See also L. Gossman, *Medievalism and the Ideologies of the Enlightenment: The World and Work of La Curne de Sainte-Pelaye* (Baltimore, 1968).

Walter Scott has been the subject of numerous biographies and studies. See, for example, J. A. Sutherland, *The Life of Walter Scott* (Oxford, 1995) and D. Brown, *Walter Scott and the Historical Imagination* (London 1979). There is an excellent bibliography in the recent edition of *Ivanhoe* by G. Tulloch (London, 2000). A. N. Wilson's *A Life of Walter Scott: The Laird of Abbotsford* (London, 2002) is noteworthy for its endorsement of Scott's vision of the Middle Ages and its consequent disparagement of modern scholarly approaches. For a thought-provoking analysis of Scott's distortion of chronology in *Ivanhoe*, see C. A. Simmons, *Reversing the Conquest: History and Myth in Nineteenth-Century British Literature* (New Brunswick, 1990). For Scott's impact on other media see P. ten-Doesschate Chu, 'Pop Culture in the Making: The Romantic Craze for History', in P. ten-Doesschate Chu and G. P. Weisberg (eds), *The Popularization of Images: Visual Culture under the July Monarchy* (Princeton, 1994), pp. 166–88; C. Gordon, 'The Illustration of Sir Walter Scott: Nineteenth-Century Enthusiasm and Adaptation', *Journal of the Warburg and Courtauld Institutes*, 34 (1971), pp. 297–317; B. S. Wright, 'Scott's Historical Novels and French Historical Painting 1815–1855', *Art Bulletin*, 63 (1981), pp. 268–87.

The story of the Eglinton Tournament is engagingly recounted in Girouard, *Return to Camelot*. See also the very readable history in I. Anstruther, *The Knight and the Umbrella: An Account of the Eglinton Tournmanent 1839* (London, 1963; repr. Gloucester, 1986), which includes some interesting contemporary illustrations and documents. Useful context on the early Victorian taste for period costume is provided by H. E. Roberts, 'Victorian Medievalism: Revival or Masquerade?', in *Browning Institute Studies*, vol. 8, ed. W. S. Patterson (New York, 1980), pp. 11–44.

For the growth of medievalism and medieval scholarship in North America, see the important article by R. Fleming, 'Picturesque History and the Medieval in Nineteenth-Century America', *American Historical Review*, 100 (1995), pp. 1061–94. There is a great deal of interest in J. Fraser, *America and the Patterns of Chivalry* (Cambridge, 1982). See also P. W. Williams, 'The Medieval Heritage in American Religious Architecture', in B. Rosenthal and P. E. Szarmach (eds), *Medievalism in American Culture* (Binghamton, NY, 1989), pp. 171–91. The darker side of the appropriation of the Middle Ages is thoughtfully explored in R. Horsman, *Race and Manifest Destiny: The Origins of American Racial Anglo-Saxonism* (Cambridge, Mass., 1981).

For Scott and the antebellum South, see R. G. Osterweis, *Romanticism and Nationalism in the Old South* (New Haven, 1949). This should, however, be read alongside B. Wyatt-Brown, *Southern Honor* (New York, 1982) and E. D. Genovese, 'The Southern Slaveholders' View of the Middle Ages', in B. Rosenthal and P. E. Szarmach (eds), *Medievalism in American Culture* (Binghamton, NY, 1989), pp. 31–52. See also the intriguing, if less than wholly convincing, remarks in L. White, 'The Legacy of the Middle Ages in the American Wild West', *Speculum*, 40 (1965), pp. 191–202.

For an accessible and beautifully illustrated history of the Vikings, see *The Oxford Illustrated History of the Vikings*, ed. P. H. Sawyer (Oxford, 1997). The chapter in this volume by L. Lönnroth, 'The Vikings in History and Legend', pp. 225–49 is an excellent account of the rediscovery and appropriation of the Vikings in modern times. See also the readable and interesting A. Wawn, *The Vikings and the Victorians: Inventing the Old North in Nineteenth-Century Britain* (Cambridge, 2000). The story of the growth of American enthusiasm for things Norse is ably told in G. Barnes, *Viking America: The First Millennium* (Cambridge, 2001), and also in her 'The Norse Discovery of America and the American Discovery of Norse (1828–1892)', in T. Shippey and M. Arnold (eds), *Appropriating the Middle Ages: Scholarship, Politics, Fraud* (Cambridge, 2001), pp. 167–88. The main sources for the original Norse discovery of America are translated by H. Pálsson and M. Magnusson in *The Vinland Sagas: The Norse Discovery of America* (Harmondsworth, 1978). For a useful collection of sources bearing on the Vikings see R. I. Page, *Chronicles of the Vikings: Records, Memorials and Myths* (London, 1995). For Tolkien, see H. Carpenter, *J. R. R. Tolkien: A Biography* (London, 1977) and P. H. Kocher, *Master of Middle-Earth: The Achievement of J. R. R. Tolkien* (London, 1973).

For debates about the Middle Ages before the nineteenth century, see, in addition to Sweet, *Antiquaries*, S. Kliger, *The Goths in England: A Study in Seventeenth and Eighteenth Century Thought* (Cambridge, Mass., 1952); L. Fox (ed.), *English Historical Scholarship in the Sixteenth and Seventeenth Centuries* (London, 1956); M. McKisack, *Medieval History in the Tudor Age* (Oxford, 1971); R. McKitterick, 'The Study of Frankish History in France and Germany in the Sixteenth and Seventeenth Centuries', *Francia*, 8 (1980), pp. 556–72; H. A. MacDougall, *Racial Myth in English History: Trojans, Teutons, and Anglo-Saxons* (Montreal, 1982); R. J. Smith, *The Gothic Bequest: Medieval Institutions in British Thought, 1688–1863* (Cambridge, 1987).

Chapter 2   What are the 'Middle Ages'?

For Abelard, see the immensely scholarly and interesting M. T. Clanchy, *Abelard: A Medieval Life* (Oxford, 1997). See also Abelard's autobiographical memoire, the *Historia Calamitatum*, in *The Letters of Abelard and Heloise*, trans. B. Radice, rev. M. T. Clanchy (Harmondsworth, 2003).

For the problems of historical periodization, there is a very thoughtful and clear discussion in L. Jordanova, *History in Practice* (London, 2000). See also G. A. Kubler, *The Shape of Time: Remarks on the History of Things* (New Haven, 1962); L. Besserman (ed.), *The Challenge of Periodization: Old Paradigms and New Perspectives* (New York, 1996); and W. Green, 'Periodization in European and World History', *Journal of World History*, 3 (1992), pp. 13–53.

The origins and merits of the terms 'medieval' and 'Middle Ages' are explored in an impressive study by T. Reuter, 'Medieval: Another Tyrannous Construct?', *Medieval History Journal*, 1 (1998), pp. 25–45. For some older but still useful discussions of the origins of the terminology, see G. Burr, 'Anent the Middle Ages', *American Historical Review*, 18 (1912–13), pp. 710–26; C. Gordon, *Medium Aevum and the Middle Ages* (Oxford, 1925); N. Edelman, 'The Early Uses of *Medium Aevum, Moyen Age*, Middle Ages' and 'Other Early Uses of *Moyen Age* and *Moyen Temps*', in his *The Eye of the Beholder: Essays in French Literature*, ed. J. Brody (Baltimore, 1974), pp. 58–85; G. Barraclough, 'Medium Aevum: Some Reflections on Mediaeval History and on the Term "The Middle Ages"', in his *History in a Changing World* (Oxford, 1957), pp. 54–63. See also the helpful overview of the subject in P. Delogu, *An Introduction to Medieval History*, trans. M. Moran (London, 2002).

The literature on the Renaissance is vast. Two very useful introductions, both with full bibliographies, are found in A. Brown, *The Renaissance*, 2nd edn (Harlow, 1999) and P. Burke, *The Renaissance*, 2nd edn (London, 1997). Joan Kelly's article 'Did Women Have a Renaissance', is in *Becoming Visible: Women in European History*, ed. R. Bridenthal, C. Koonz and S. M. Stuard, 2nd edn (Boston, 1987), pp. 175–201. The most accessible translation of Burckhardt's masterpiece is *The Civilization of the Renaissance in Italy*, trans. S. G. C. Middlemore, with introduction by P. Burke and notes by P. Murray (Harmondsworth, 1990). For Alberti, see his *On Painting*, trans. C. Grayson with an introduction by M. Kemp (Harmondsworth, 1991). For Vasari, see his *Lives of the Artists: A Selection*, trans. G. Bull, 2 vols. (Harmondsworth, 1987).

For the Monumenta, see, in addition to Delogu, *Introduction*, D. Knowles, 'The *Monumenta Germaniae Historica*', in his *Great Historical Enterprises: Problems in Monastic History* (London, 1963), pp. 63–97.

Columbus' account of his travels is in Christopher Columbus, *The Four Voyages*, trans. J. M. Cohen (Harmondsworth, 1969).

Henri Pirenne's famous thesis about the end of the Roman world is found in his *Mohammed and Charlemagne*, trans. B. Miall (London, 1939). This has been much debated and revised: see, for example, A. F. Havighurst (ed.), *The Pirenne Thesis: Analysis, Criticism and Revision*, 3rd edn (Lexington, Mass., 1976); and R. Hodges and D. Whitehouse, *Mohammed, Charlemagne and the Origins of Europe: Archaeology and the Pirenne Thesis* (London, 1983). For a clear and up-to-date survey of the emergence of the early medieval world, see R. Collins, *Early Medieval Europe, 300–1000*, 2nd edn (Basingstoke, 1999).

For the extension of 'medieval' to non-European settings, see, for example, R. Oliver and A. Atmore, *Medieval Africa, 1250–1800* (Cambridge, 2001); R. K. Verma, *Feudal Social Formation in Early Medieval India* (New Delhi, 2002); and K. F. Friday, *Samurai, Warfare and the State in Early Medieval Japan* (London, 2003).

There is a lively discussion of the Sixties in A. Marwick, *The Sixties: Cultural Revolution in Britain, France, Italy, and the United States, c.1958–c.1974* (Oxford, 1998). For a Sixties radical's memories of the period, see Tariq Ali's *Street Fighting Years: An Autobiography of the Sixties* (London, 1987).

A clear and helpful introduction to feudalism in its broad cultural setting is to be found in C. B. Bouchard, *Strong of Body, Brave, and Noble: Chivalry and Society in Medieval France* (Ithaca, NY, 1998). Marc Bloch's classic book has been translated as *Feudal Society* by L. A. Manyon (London 1961). Bloch's life and academic career are interestingly studied in C. Fink, *Marc Bloch: A Life* (Cambridge, 1989). Peggy Brown's seminal article 'The Tyranny of a Construct: Feudalism and Historians of Medieval Europe' first appeared in *American Historical Review*, 79 (1974), pp. 1063–88 and is conveniently reprinted in L. K. Little and B. H. Rosenwein (eds), *Debating the Middle Ages: Issues and Readings* (Oxford, 1998), pp. 148–69. See also S. Reynolds, *Fiefs and Vassals: The Medieval Evidence Reinterpreted* (Oxford, 1994).

Chapter 3   The Evidence for the Middle Ages

For an up-to-date and informative survey of the nature of primary sources and their applications, with much of direct relevance to the study of medieval history, see M. Howell and W. Prevenier, *From Reliable Sources: An Introduction to Historical Methods* (Ithaca, NY, 2001). There is a full survey of the sources available to medievalists in R. C. van Caenegem, *Guide to the Sources of Medieval History* (Amsterdam, 1978). Many of the main types of sources are discussed in more technical detail in J. M. Powell (ed.), *Medieval Studies: An Introduction*, 2nd edn (Syracuse, NY, 1992).

Mabillon's career is described in R. Avis, 'Jean Mabillon (1632–1707)', in H. Damico and J. B. Zavadil (eds), *Medieval Scholarship: Biographical Studies on the Formation of a Discipline. I: History* (New York, 1995), pp. 15–32. This volume also contains many other helpful essays on the founding figures of academic medieval history. The work of the Maurists is magisterially surveyed in D. Knowles, 'The Maurists', in his *Great Historical Enterprises: Problems in Monastic History* (London, 1963), pp. 33–62.

For the Courtois forgeries, see D. Abulafia, 'Invented Italians in the Courtois Charters', in P. W. Edbury (ed.), *Crusade and Settlement* (Cardiff, 1985), pp. 135–43; R.-H. Bautier, 'Forgeries et falsifications de documents par un officine généalogique au milieu du XIXe siècle', *Bibliothèque de l'Ecole des Chartes*, 132 (1974), pp. 75–94. For a valuable study of medieval forgers in action, see A. Hiatt, *The Making of Medieval Forgeries: False Documents in Fifteenth-Century England* (London, 2004).

Michael Clanchy's ground-breaking work on medieval records is to be found in his *From Memory to Written Record: England 1066–1307*, 2nd edn (Oxford, 1993). Orderic Vitalis's important twelfth-century history has been edited as *The Ecclesiastical History*, ed. and trans. M. Chibnall, 6 vols. (Oxford, 1969–80). See also M. Chibnall, *The World of Orderic Vitalis* (Oxford, 1984). Geoffrey of Vigeois awaits a detailed modern study: see M. Aubrun, 'Le Prieur Geoffroy de Vigeois et sa chronique', *Revue Mabillon*, 58 (1974), pp. 313–26. For Aethelweard, see his *Chronicle*, ed. A. Campbell (Edinburgh, 1962), and for Asser *Alfred the Great: Asser's Life of King Alfred and other Contemporary Sources*, trans. S. Keynes and M. Lapidge (Harmondsworth, 1983).

The story of the destruction of the Naples archive is told in R. Filangieri, *L'Archivio di Stato di Napoli durante la Seconda Guerra Mondiale*, ed. S. Palmieri (Naples, 1996). An English version of the report by Count Filangieri, who was responsible for the archive at the time of its destruction, is in *The American Archivist*, 7 (1944), pp. 252–5, reproduced at <http:/www.kakarigi.net/manu/ preced.htm#Naples1>. There is also a helpful, brief account of the affair in D. Abulafia, *Frederick II: A Medieval Emperor* (London, 1988). The Bayeux Tapestry's chequered past is chronicled in S. Brown, *The Bayeux Tapestry: History and Bibliography* (Woodbridge, 1988). For the close shaves in the 1790s, see M. Pezet, 'Rapport fait au Conseil municipal de Bayeux au nom de la Commission chargée de prendre des mesures pour la conservation de la Tapisserie de la reine Mathilde', *Bulletin Monumental*, 6 (1840), pp. 62–79.

For the two most famous examples of sixteenth-century microhistory, see N. Z. Davis, *The Return of Martin Guerre* (Cambridge, Mass., 1983) and C. Ginzburg, *The Cheese and the Worms: The Cosmos of a Sixteenth-Century Miller*, trans. J. and A. Tedeschi (London, 1980). Also of interest as another classic of the genre, though set later in time, is R. Darnton, 'Workers' Revolt: The Great Cat Massacre of the Rue Saint-Séverin', in his *The Great Cat Massacre and Other Episodes in French Cultural History* (London, 2001), pp. 74–104. For a survey of the impact and significance of microhistory in general, see G. Levi, 'On Microhistory', in P. Burke (ed.), *New Perspectives on Historical Writing*, 2nd edn. (Cambridge, 2001), pp. 97–119. Emmanuel Le Roy Ladurie's bestseller about the fourteenth-century Pyrenean village is published in English as *Montaillou: Cathars and Catholics in a French Village, 1294–1324*, trans. B. Bray (London, 1978).

The Córdoba martyrs are the subject of two recent studies which offer different interpretations: K. B. Wolf, *Christian Martyrs in Muslim Spain* (Cambridge, 1988); and J. A. Coope, *The Martyrs of Córdoba: Community and Family Conflict in an Age of Mass Conversion* (Lincoln, Nebraska, 1995). The writings of Eulogius and

Paulus Alvarus are examined in detail in E. P. Colbert, *The Martyrs of Córdoba (850–859): A Study of the Sources* (Washington, DC, 1962). For general background, see R. Collins, *Early Medieval Spain: Unity in Diversity, 400–1000*, 2nd edn (Basingstoke, 1995).

For Galbert of Bruges, see *The Murder of Charles the Good*, trans. J. B. Ross (New York, 1959; repr. Toronto, 1982). There is a detailed and convincing analysis of the text in J. Rider, *God's Scribe: The Historiographical Art of Galbert of Bruges* (Washington, DC, 2001).

The theory of the perception of time applied at the end of this chapter is drawn from the discussion in D. Carr, *Time, Narrative, and History* (Bloomington, Indiana, 1986). The question of narrativity and history has spawned an extensive literature in recent years. A very helpful point of entry, which includes readings from the work of the main scholars who have contributed to the debate, is G. Roberts (ed.), *The History and Narrative Reader* (London, 2001).

Chapter 4   Is Medieval History Relevant?

Patrick Geary's *The Myth of Nations: The Medieval Origins of Europe* (Princeton, 2002) is a thought-provoking study which examines the ways in which medieval history has been mobilized and misappropriated in recent times. For the modern reincarnation of the Lombard League, see the perceptive comments of Edward Coleman in 'Bossi's Lega Nord – History and Myth' at <http://www.threemonkeysonline.com/threemon_printable.php?id=7>. See also the same author's 'The Lombard League: Myth and History', in H. B. Clarke and J. Devlin (eds), *European Encounters: Essays in Memory of Arthur Lovett* (Dublin, 2003). For the Middle Ages in Franco's Spain, see the account of the career of the medievalist Ramón Menéndez Pidal in R. A. Fletcher, *The Quest for El Cid* (London, 1989).

There are many good histories of the English language. The erudite and readable David Crystal has penned a number of useful works: see his *The English Language*, 2nd edn (London, 2002) and *The Stories of English* (London, 2004). There is a great deal of interest in G. Hughes, *A History of English Words* (Oxford, 1999). Though now a little dated, the classic treatment by Simeon Potter, *Our Language*, rev. edn (Harmondsworth, 1976) remains valuable. For the global expansion of English see D. Crystal, *English as a Global Language* (Cambridge, 1997). For the wider context see P. Wolff, *Western Languages, A.D. 100–1500*, trans. F. Partridge (London, 1971; repr. London, 2003). A useful point of comparison is French, for which see P. Rickard, *A History of the French Language*, 2nd edn (London, 1989). For Frisian, see R. H. Bremmer, 'Late Medieval and Early Modern Opinions of the Affinity between English and Frisian: The Growth of a Commonplace', *Folia Linguistica Historica*, 9 (1989), pp. 167–91.

For the best definition and succinct discussion of the crusades, see J. S. C. Riley-Smith, *What were the Crusades?*, 3rd edn (Basingstoke, 2002). An interesting discussion of crusading seen through the prism of some well-known primary sources is N. J. Housley, *The Crusaders* (Stroud, 2002), the concluding chapter of which has some thoughtful and measured remarks on the relationship between the medieval crusades and current affairs. C. J. Tyerman, *The Invention of the Crusades* (Basingstoke, 1998) has a useful chapter on crusade historiography since the sixteenth century, though some of its views on very recent historians are sententious. For some post-medieval views of the crusade, see the rich body of material assembled in E. Siberry, *The New Crusaders: Images of the Crusades in the Nineteenth and Early Twentieth Centuries* (Aldershot, 2000), which may be profitably read in conjunction with A. Knobler, 'Saint Louis and French Political Culture', in L. J. Workman and K. Verduin (eds), *Medievalism in Europe II* (Studies in Medievalism, 8; Woodbridge, 1997), pp. 156–73; and K. Mulholland, 'Michaud's History of the Crusades and the French Crusade in Algeria under Louis-Philippe', in P. ten-Doesschate Chu and G. P. Weisberg (eds), *The Popularization of Images: Visual Culture under the July Monarchy* (Princeton, 1994), pp. 144–65. For Islamic views, the fundamental work is C. Hillenbrand, *The Crusades: Islamic Perspectives* (Edinburgh, 1999), which includes a very judicious discussion of the memory of the crusades in modern Islam. See also. R. Urwin, 'Islam and the Crusades, 1096–1699', in J. S. C. Riley-Smith (ed.), *The Oxford Illustrated History of the Crusades* (Oxford, 1995), pp. 217–59 and the same author's 'Saladin and the Third Crusade: A Case Study in Historiography and the Historical Novel', in M. Bentley (ed.), *Companion to Historiography* (London, 1997), pp. 139–52. For a salutary take on the whole notion of McWorld vs. Jihad, see F. Wheen, *How Mumbo-Jumbo Conquered the World: A Short History of Delusions* (London, 2004).

For the *taifas* and the Almoravids in Spain, see A. Mackay, *Spain in the Middle Ages: From Frontier to Empire, 1000–1500* (London, 1977); R. A. Fletcher, *Moorish Spain* (London, 1992); H. N. Kennedy, *Muslim Spain and Portugal: A Political History of al-Andalus* (London, 1996).

There is a concise and helpful account of the rise and impact of cultural history in M. Rubin, 'What is Cultural History Now?', in D. Cannadine (ed.), *What is History Now?* (Basingstoke, 2002), pp. 80–94. The contribution of French historians to the study of *mentalités* is explained in P. Burke, *The French Historical Revolution: The Annales School, 1929–89* (Cambridge, 1990). For Jean-Claude Schmitt's analysis of the cult of St Guinefort, see his *The Holy Greyhound: Guinefort, Healer of Children since the Thirteenth Century*, trans. M. Thom (Cambridge, 1983).

Index